The Sindhi Lai  ιey
Throu

Azhar ul Haque Sario

Unveiling the Sindhi Language: A Historical Tapestry

Unveiling the Secrets of Proto-Sindhi: A Journey Through Time

Imagine Sindh as a vibrant tapestry woven with threads of diverse linguistic influences. Before the arrival of Islam, this land echoed with a language that has faded into the mists of time – Proto-Sindhi. Like skilled archaeologists, linguists carefully sift through the sands of history, piecing together the fragments of this ancient tongue.

Comparative Linguistics: Tracing the Family Tree

Think of languages as branches on a vast family tree. By comparing Sindhi to its "cousins" like Sanskrit, Punjabi, and Gujarati, we can trace their shared ancestry back to Proto-Sindhi. This process, known as comparative linguistics, is like a linguistic detective game, where researchers identify common words and sounds to reconstruct the ancestral language.

But the story doesn't end there. Sindhi also bears the imprint of Dravidian languages like Tamil and Telugu. These languages, spoken by ancient communities in the region, have left their mark on Sindhi's vocabulary and grammar. It's as if Proto-Sindhi, in its journey through time, embraced these influences, creating a unique linguistic blend.

Archaeological Evidence: Whispers from the Past

The Indus script, a mysterious writing system from the ancient Indus Valley Civilization, tantalizes researchers with its secrets. While it remains undeciphered, it offers glimpses into the cultural and linguistic practices of the time. Imagine these symbols as puzzle pieces, waiting to be assembled into a coherent picture of Proto-Sindhi.

Early inscriptions in the Brahmi script, like ancient whispers, provide further clues. These fragments, etched on stone or pottery, offer snapshots of Sindhi's evolution, revealing how its sounds and grammar changed over time.

Reconstructing the Proto-Sindhi Verb System: Breathing Life into the Past

Through meticulous analysis, linguists have begun to reconstruct the verb system of Proto-Sindhi. Imagine this process as bringing a forgotten melody back to life. By studying modern Sindhi dialects and early inscriptions, researchers have identified patterns and variations that point to the structure of the ancestral language.

Dravidian Influences: A Cultural Tapestry

The presence of Dravidian features In Sindhi suggests a rich history of cultural exchange. It's as if two ancient communities, speaking different languages, came together, sharing their words, sounds, and even grammatical structures. This linguistic fusion has created a unique tapestry, reflecting the diversity and interconnectedness of the region's past.

Early Inscriptions: Echoes of Change

Early inscriptions in the Brahmi script serve as time capsules, preserving snapshots of Sindhi's evolution. By studying these inscriptions, researchers can trace the gradual changes in the language's sounds, words, and grammar. It's like watching a language transform over time, adapting to new influences and cultural shifts.

Digital Reconstruction: Reviving a Lost Language

Imagine a digital platform where learners can immerse themselves in the world of Proto-Sindhi. This interactive tool, created through the efforts of researchers, would provide a comprehensive resource for studying the language's history and evolution. It's as if we're breathing new life into a forgotten tongue, allowing future generations to connect with their linguistic heritage.

Conclusion: A Tapestry of Time

The reconstruction of Proto-Sindhi is a journey through time, a quest to uncover the linguistic secrets of ancient Sindh. By combining the tools of comparative linguistics, archaeology, and inscription analysis, researchers are piecing together the fragments of this lost language. This endeavor not only sheds light on the history of Sindhi but also enriches our understanding of the region's cultural heritage. It's a reminder that languages are not static entities but living, evolving expressions of human connection and creativity.

The Persian and Arabic Tapestry Woven into Sindhi

The echoes of ancient civilizations reverberate through the Sindhi language, a testament to the rich cultural and linguistic exchange that has shaped its evolution. As Islam spread across the region, so too did the influence of Arabic and Persian, leaving an indelible mark on Sindhi's phonology, script, vocabulary, syntax, and literary traditions.

A Symphony of Sounds: Phonological Shifts

The very sounds of Sindhi were transformed by the infusion of Arabic and Persian. New consonant clusters, such as the "kt" in "kitaab" (book) and the "lm" in "qalam" (pen), became integral to the language's phonetic landscape. Vowel sounds, too, were enriched, with the introduction of "i" in "dil" (heart) and "o" in "aakhon" (eyes). These phonetic innovations not only added complexity but also enhanced the language's expressive power.

A Written Legacy: Script Adaptation

The Arabic script, a vessel of Islamic knowledge and culture, was adapted to accommodate the unique sounds of Sindhi. New letters were introduced to represent sounds absent in the original Arabic script, such as "jha," "gha," "cha," "dha," and "pha." Diacritical marks, known as "zabar," "pesh," and "zair," were developed to indicate vowel sounds and other phonetic nuances. This adaptation allowed Sindhi to flourish as a written language, preserving its rich literary heritage.

A Tapestry of Words: Vocabulary Enrichment

Countless words from Arabic and Persian were woven into the fabric of Sindhi vocabulary. From the sacred verses of the Quran to the elegant poetry of Persian poets, a vast array of words enriched the language. This linguistic borrowing not only expanded Sindhi's expressive range but also connected it to the broader Islamic world.

A Syntactic Embrace: Grammatical Influence

The influence of Arabic and Persian extended beyond vocabulary to the very structure of Sindhi sentences. Sentence structures were often modeled on Arabic and Persian patterns, and grammatical constructions were borrowed to enhance the language's precision and clarity.

A Literary Renaissance: Stylistic Innovation

The literary landscape of Sindh was transformed by Arabic and Persian influences. Epic poems like the "Shah Jo Risalo" were composed in styles reminiscent of Persian epics, while poets embraced Arabic and Persian poetic forms like the ghazal and masnavi. This infusion of literary styles fostered a rich and diverse literary tradition.

A Linguistic Legacy: The Etymological Quest

To fully appreciate the depth of the Arabic and Persian imprint on Sindhi, a comprehensive etymological dictionary is essential. Such a dictionary would illuminate the origins and meanings of Sindhi words, tracing their evolution through time. It would serve as an invaluable resource for scholars, students, and language enthusiasts alike.

In conclusion, the intricate interplay between Sindhi, Arabic, and Persian has resulted in a language of extraordinary richness and beauty. By understanding the historical and linguistic forces that shaped Sindhi, we can better appreciate its unique character and its enduring legacy.

The British colonial era in Sindh (1843-1947) significantly impacted the Sindhi language, leading to both standardization and new literary styles.

Standardization of Sindhi

The British colonial administration played a crucial role in standardizing the Sindhi language. They established educational institutions, introduced a standardized script (Devanagari), and conducted language surveys to collect and analyze different dialects. These efforts led to the codification of Sindhi grammar and vocabulary, laying the foundation for the modern standard language.

Key figures and events:

George Smith: A British civil servant who compiled a comprehensive dictionary of Sindhi words, The Dictionary of the Sindhi Language.
Ernest Trumpp: A German scholar who published The Grammar of the Sindhi Language Compared with the Sanskrit-Prakrit and Cognate Indian Vernaculars, considered a landmark work in Sindhi linguistics.

Sindhi Sahitya Sabha: A literary society founded in 1918 that played a significant role in promoting Sindhi literature and culture.

Impact of standardization:

The standardization of Sindhi facilitated the development of a common literary language, which helped to unite the diverse Sindhi-speaking population. It also led to the emergence of a new generation of writers and poets who explored different themes and styles.

Contributions of Missionaries and Scholars

Missionaries and scholars, particularly those associated with Christian missions, also made significant contributions to the development of Sindhi literature and linguistics. They translated religious texts into Sindhi, published grammars and dictionaries, and established schools and colleges.

Key figures and institutions:

American Presbyterian Mission: Established in 1843, the mission played a crucial role in promoting education and literacy in Sindh.

Church Missionary Society: Established in 1855, the society also contributed to the development of Sindhi literature and education.

Sindh Madressatul Islam: A prominent Islamic educational institution founded in 1924, which played a key role in promoting Sindhi language and culture.

Impact of missionaries and scholars:

The contributions of missionaries and scholars helped to expand the corpus of Sindhi literature and broaden its readership. They also introduced new literary genres and styles, such as the novel and the short story.

Emergence of New Literary Genres and Styles

During the colonial period, new literary genres and styles emerged in Sindhi, reflecting the changing social and political landscape. These included the novel, the short story, the essay, and the poem.

Key figures and works:

Mirza Qaleech Beg: A prominent Sindhi poet who wrote in the classical style, but also experimented with new forms and themes.

Ghulam Muhammad Shah: A leading figure in the development of Sindhi prose, who wrote novels, short stories, and essays.

Mumtaz Bhutto: A poet and playwright who wrote about social and political issues.

Shah Abdul Latif Bhittai: A Sufi poet whose work continues to be popular today.

Impact of new literary genres and styles:

The emergence of new literary genres and styles helped to revitalize Sindhi literature and make it more relevant to modern audiences. It also allowed Sindhi writers to express their views on social and political issues and to challenge traditional values.

Practical Application: Developing Language Teaching Materials

The study of the colonial period in Sindh can provide valuable insights into the development of the Sindhi language and its literary traditions. This knowledge can be incorporated into language teaching materials to help learners understand the historical and cultural context of the language.

Here are some specific examples of how historical context and linguistic evolution can be incorporated into language teaching materials:

Historical overviews: Provide students with an overview of the history of Sindh, including the colonial period. This will help them to understand the sociopolitical context in which the language developed.

Linguistic evolution: Trace the evolution of the Sindhi language from its earliest roots to the present day. This will help students to understand how the language has changed over time and to appreciate the diversity of its dialects.

Literary genres and styles: Introduce students to different literary genres and styles that have developed in Sindhi. This will help them to appreciate the richness and diversity of Sindhi literature.

Cultural references: Incorporate cultural references into language teaching materials. This will help students to develop a deeper understanding of the Sindhi language and culture.

By incorporating historical context and linguistic evolution into language teaching materials, we can help students to develop a more comprehensive understanding of the Sindhi language and its place in the world.

Sindhi in the 21st Century: A Tapestry of Tradition and Technology

Imagine a vibrant tapestry, threads of ancient Sindhi interweaving with the bright hues of modern technology. That's the story of Sindhi in the 21st century – a dynamic dance between tradition and innovation.

Globalization, like a powerful wind, has swept across the world, carrying with it both challenges and opportunities for languages like Sindhi. While the dominance of English and Urdu might seem like storm clouds threatening to overshadow Sindhi, the language, like a sturdy tree, has deep roots. It thrives in the heart of homes, in the warmth of community gatherings, and whispers through the bustling streets of Sindh.

Yet, the winds of change are undeniable. Code-switching, once a subtle undercurrent, now flows openly through conversations, blending Sindhi with Urdu and English like colors in a painter's palette. A young Sindhi student might discuss the latest cricket match in a vibrant mix of Sindhi and Urdu, seamlessly switching between languages, reflecting the multicultural world they inhabit.

But fear not, for technology, like a master weaver, offers new threads to strengthen the Sindhi tapestry. Online dictionaries and language learning apps become vibrant threads, connecting learners worldwide. Imagine a young girl in Karachi learning Sindhi through a game on her phone, her laughter echoing the joy of discovery.

Digital archives safeguard ancient Sindhi texts like precious jewels, preserving stories and songs for generations to come. Picture a scholar in London accessing a centuries-old Sindhi manuscript with a few clicks, unlocking the wisdom of the past.

Social media, a bustling marketplace of ideas, becomes a stage for Sindhi. Hashtags like #SindhiPride trend on Twitter, while Facebook groups buzz with discussions on Sindhi literature and poetry. A young musician in Hyderabad uploads his latest Sindhi song on YouTube, garnering thousands of views and sparking a cultural revival.

But the tapestry is not static; it evolves. Informal language flourishes online, emojis adding emotional flourishes to

Sindhi text messages, and new words emerge to capture the digital age. A lively debate unfolds on a Sindhi forum about the best way to translate "internet meme" into Sindhi, showcasing the language's adaptability.

To truly engage the younger generation, we need to weave technology into the fabric of Sindhi learning. Imagine a gamified app where players embark on a virtual quest through the historical sites of Sindh, learning Sindhi words and phrases as they solve puzzles and interact with colorful characters.

Social media campaigns could challenge users to share their favorite Sindhi proverbs or create short videos showcasing their talents in Sindhi. Picture a popular Sindhi vlogger hosting a live online poetry slam, inspiring young people to express themselves in their mother tongue.

Digital storytelling platforms could empower young Sindhis to create and share animated stories, comics, or even dub popular cartoons in Sindhi, giving them a voice and ownership in the digital world.

And who knows, maybe one day we'll explore the ruins of Mohenjo-daro through a virtual reality experience, guided by a Sindhi-speaking avatar, bringing history to life through the magic of technology.

The future of Sindhi is a tapestry woven with threads of tradition, innovation, and the boundless energy of its speakers. By embracing both the enduring strength of its heritage and the transformative power of technology, Sindhi can flourish in the 21st century and beyond.

The Art of Writing Sindhi: A Journey Through Scripts

Khudabadi: A Forgotten Script's Fight for Survival

Imagine a language, a unique script, whispered through the ages, its echoes fading with each passing generation. Khudabadi, a script born in the vibrant city of Khudabad, Sindh, is such a language. A descendant of the ancient Brahmi script, it once adorned manuscripts and inscriptions, narrating the tales of the Lohana community and other Hindu and Muslim groups of Sindh.

Unveiling the Past: The Delicate Art of Deciphering Khudabadi

To understand Khudabadi, one must delve into the intricate world of paleography. Scholars, akin to linguistic detectives, meticulously examine the physical characteristics of the script - the shape of letters, their spacing, the ink's age - to piece together the puzzle. By comparing it to its ancestral script, Brahmi, and other scripts like Devanagari, they unravel the secrets hidden within the fading ink. Contextual clues, like the subject matter and historical period, further aid in this delicate process.

Dr. Ghulam Ali Allana, a renowned Pakistani scholar, has made significant contributions to the study of Khudabadi. His comprehensive research, published in 1983, offers a deep dive into the script's history, evolution, and regional variations.

A Script's Journey Through Time: Regional Variations and Historical Development

Khudabadi's roots trace back to the 3rd century BCE when the Brahmi script first arrived in Sindh. Over centuries, it adapted to the nuances of the Sindhi language, eventually blossoming into the distinct Khudabadi script.

Just like human languages evolve with diverse dialects, Khudabadi too developed regional variations. The Shikaripuri script, with its elegant calligraphy and abundant vowel markers, emerged from the city of Shikarpur. The Dadu Panthi script, used by the followers of the 16th-century saint Dadu Dayal, is characterized by its unique ligatures and spiritual symbolism.

The Silent Script: Reasons for Decline and Challenges in Revival

The 19th century marked the beginning of Khudabadi's decline. The British colonial era favored the Arabic-based Sindhi script, gradually eclipsing the indigenous script. Factors like increasing literacy rates and the advent of modern technologies further accelerated the decline.

Reviving Khudabadi is a monumental task. The scarcity of fluent readers and writers, coupled with the absence of a standardized orthography, poses significant challenges. However, dedicated organizations and individuals are working tirelessly to preserve this linguistic heritage. They are developing educational materials, promoting its use in daily life, and safeguarding the precious manuscripts and inscriptions.

A Digital Renaissance: Bringing Khudabadi into the Modern Era

To make Khudabadi accessible to a wider audience, digital tools are proving to be invaluable. The development of digital fonts and keyboards is a crucial step in this direction. These tools empower people to type and read Khudabadi on computers, smartphones, and other electronic devices.

A Legacy Worth Preserving

Khudabadi, a testament to the rich cultural heritage of Sindh, deserves to be celebrated and preserved. It is a reminder of the resilience of language and the enduring power of human creativity. By understanding and appreciating this forgotten script, we honor the past and pave the way for a brighter future for Khudabadi.

The Sindhi Script: A Tapestry of Language, Culture, and Art

In the heart of Sindh, where the mighty Indus River carves its path through the land, a unique script blossoms, a testament to the resilience and creativity of its people. The Sindhi script, an exquisite adaptation of the Perso-Arabic script, is a story etched in ink, a journey through language, culture, and art.

A Dance of Adaptation

Imagine a script that pirouettes and twirls, adapting to the rhythm of a new language. When the Perso-Arabic script first arrived in Sindh, carried by the winds of the Arab conquest in the 8th century, it encountered a language brimming with sounds it couldn't quite capture. Sindhi, with its playful implosives, its graceful retroflexes, and its resonant nasals, demanded more.

And so, the script transformed, like a chameleon changing its colors. Sindhi scholars and writers, the choreographers of this linguistic dance, added new letters, adorned existing ones with diacritical marks, and modified others, creating a script that mirrored the nuances of Sindhi pronunciation.

The Script's Symphony

The Sindhi script is a symphony of letters and diacritical marks, each playing a vital role in the melody of the language. New letters emerged, like the implosives ڎ, ڃ, ٻ, and ڳ, the retroflexes ڙ, ٽ, ٿ, and ڊ, and the nasals ڱ, ڃ, and ڻ, each adding a unique note to the symphony. Diacritical marks, like delicate ornaments, embellished existing letters, distinguishing between similar sounds and adding depth to vowel qualities.

This expanded repertoire of characters became the voice of Sindhi literature, allowing poets to weave verses that captured the soul of the language and writers to craft stories that resonated with the hearts of the people.

Standardization: A Bridge to Literacy

Like a river finding its course, the Sindhi script meandered through time, evolving organically, creating dialects and variations in spelling and pronunciation. To bridge these differences and foster literacy, standardization efforts began in the early 20th century.

Spelling standards were established, dictionaries and grammars were compiled, and literacy programs were launched, uniting the Sindhi people under a common script. This standardization paved the way for increased literacy rates, making Sindhi literature accessible to all and strengthening the language's role in education and administration.

Calligraphy: The Art of the Soul

In the hands of Sindhi calligraphers, the script transcends mere communication, becoming an art form that expresses the soul of the people. With elegant curves and flowing lines, the script adorns mosques, tombs, manuscripts, and everyday objects, transforming them into works of art.

Sindhi calligraphy, influenced by both Islamic and regional traditions, boasts a variety of styles, each with its own distinctive character. Nastaliq, with its graceful curves, Naskh, with its clarity and boldness, and Thuluth, with its intricate patterns, all contribute to the rich tapestry of Sindhi calligraphy.

A Guide to Unveiling the Art

Imagine a guide that unlocks the secrets of Sindhi calligraphy, a key to understanding its history, techniques, and cultural significance. This comprehensive guide would delve into the origins and evolution of the script, explore its various styles, and provide practical guidance on mastering the art.

It would be a treasure trove for learners and enthusiasts, a bridge connecting them to the rich cultural heritage of Sindh. It would also serve as a beacon, illuminating the path for future generations to carry on this beautiful tradition.

Conclusion: A Legacy Etched in Ink

The Sindhi script is a testament to the ingenuity and resilience of the Sindhi people. It is a script that has adapted, evolved, and flourished, preserving a unique linguistic heritage and fostering a vibrant literary tradition.

Through standardization efforts and the promotion of literacy, the script has become a cornerstone of Sindhi identity, uniting its people and strengthening its culture. And through the art of calligraphy, the script transcends its functional role, becoming an expression of the soul, a reflection of the aesthetic sensibilities and spiritual values of the Sindhi people.

The Sindhi script is a legacy etched in ink, a story that continues to unfold, carrying with it the hopes, dreams, and aspirations of a people. It is a story that deserves to be celebrated, preserved, and shared with the world.

Devanagari: A Cultural Crossroads

A Tale of Two Scripts

The Sindhi language, a vibrant tapestry woven with threads of history and culture, has had a complex relationship with its scripts. For centuries, the Perso-Arabic script was its primary vehicle, a testament to the region's Islamic heritage. However, the partition of India in 1947 marked a turning point, especially for Sindhi speakers in India.

A New Dawn, A New Script

The Indian government, in its pursuit of national integration, encouraged the adoption of Devanagari, the script of Hindi, for various regional languages. Sindhi was one such language. While this move aimed to unify the nation linguistically, it sparked a debate within the Sindhi community.

A Clash of Cultures

For many Sindhi Hindus, Devanagari offered a connection to the broader Indian cultural landscape. It was seen as a way to bridge linguistic divides and foster a sense of national belonging. However, for Muslim Sindhis, the shift to Devanagari felt like a departure from their Islamic heritage. The Perso-Arabic script, deeply intertwined with their religious and literary traditions, was a source of pride and identity.

The Writer's Dilemma

Imagine a young Sindhi poet, torn between tradition and modernity. They grew up reading and writing in the elegant curves of the Perso-Arabic script. Now, they're expected to adapt to the angular forms of Devanagari. It's like learning to write with a different hand, a challenge that requires both technical skill and emotional adjustment.

A Language Reborn

Despite the initial resistance, Devanagari gradually gained acceptance among Sindhi speakers in India. A new generation of writers emerged, crafting beautiful poetry and prose in the Devanagari script. While the transition wasn't without its challenges, it also opened up new possibilities for the Sindhi language.

The Digital Age and Beyond

In the digital age, the internet has become a powerful tool for language preservation and revitalization. Sindhi language enthusiasts, both in India and Pakistan, are using online platforms to connect, share, and create. Devanagari, with its compatibility with digital technologies, has played a significant role in this digital renaissance.

However, the challenge of standardization and digitization remains. While Devanagari has made significant strides, there's still a need for comprehensive digital fonts and tools to support the language.

A Legacy Endures

The adoption of Devanagari for Sindhi is a testament to the language's resilience and adaptability. It's a story of cultural evolution, a journey from tradition to modernity. While the debate over scripts may continue, one thing is certain: the Sindhi language, in all its forms, will continue to enrich the cultural tapestry of the Indian subcontinent.

The digital age has unleashed a torrent of information, connecting the world in ways never before imagined. 1 Yet, amidst this sea of data, the whispers of ancient scripts like Sindhi's Khudabadi risk being drowned out. But fear not! Technology, the very force that threatens to overshadow these treasures, also holds the key to their vibrant revival.

1. How the digital age is changing everything we know Imagine a world where Sindhi manuscripts, long hidden in dusty archives, spring to life on our screens. With the magic of OCR, these texts can be "read" by computers, unlocking their secrets for researchers and the public alike. Picture this:

A scholar in London unearths a rare Khudabadi poem with a few keystrokes, searching through a vast digital library of Sindhi literature.

A student in Karachi deciphers an ancient inscription on a crumbling monument, aided by AI-powered translation tools.

A calligrapher in Hyderabad rediscovers the beauty of their ancestral script through an online course, connecting with a global community of learners.

This is the promise of digital preservation and innovation for Sindhi scripts.

Let's delve deeper into this exciting realm:

1. Digital Tools and Resources:

OCR for Khudabadi: Imagine software that deciphers the elegant curves and intricate dots of this historical script, making centuries-old texts searchable and accessible. This is no easy feat, but with AI and machine learning, it's within our grasp.

Online Calligraphy Courses: No longer confined to physical classrooms, the art of Sindhi calligraphy can now flourish online. Interactive lessons, virtual practice sessions, and personalized feedback will empower a new generation of calligraphers worldwide.

Digital Archives: A treasure trove of Sindhi manuscripts, scattered across libraries and private collections, can be united in a virtual space. Imagine a comprehensive online archive, where researchers and enthusiasts can explore, analyze, and marvel at these cultural gems.

2. The Power of AI:

Advanced Script Recognition: AI algorithms can be trained to recognize even the most challenging handwriting, ensuring that every Sindhi script is preserved and understood.

Text Analysis and Translation: Unraveling the nuances of Sindhi poetry, identifying literary styles, and even generating new verses – AI can be a powerful tool for understanding and appreciating Sindhi literature.

Innovative Learning Tools: From interactive apps to personalized tutoring systems, AI can revolutionize how we learn Sindhi scripts and language, making the process engaging and accessible for all.

3. Social Media as a Catalyst:

Raising Awareness: Social media platforms can become vibrant hubs for celebrating Sindhi scripts, sharing their history, and showcasing their beauty.

Promoting Script Usage: Imagine a resurgence of Sindhi scripts in online communication, as people proudly use them in their posts, messages, and creative expressions.

Building Online Communities: Social media can connect Sindhi speakers, learners, and enthusiasts worldwide, fostering a sense of shared identity and purpose.

4. A Vision for the Future: The Digital Archive of Sindhi Manuscripts (DASM)

Imagine a collaborative project, bringing together institutions and individuals from across the globe to create a comprehensive digital archive of Sindhi manuscripts. DASM would be a beacon of preservation and innovation, offering:

High-quality images and metadata: Every manuscript digitized with meticulous care, accompanied by detailed information about its script, date, author, and subject matter.

Multilingual support: Accessible to users in Sindhi, English, and other languages, breaking down barriers and fostering global understanding.

Advanced search and analysis tools: Empowering researchers with powerful tools to explore the collection, analyze texts, and uncover new insights.

AI-powered features: From automated transcription to text analysis and visualization, AI can enhance the archive's capabilities and unlock the full potential of the collection.

Public engagement: Online exhibitions, workshops, and interactive features will bring the archive to life, inspiring a new generation to appreciate and cherish Sindhi heritage.

DASM is not just a dream; it's a call to action. By harnessing the power of technology and embracing collaboration, we can ensure that Sindhi scripts thrive in the digital age, their beauty and wisdom illuminating the world for generations to come.

Unearthing Sindh's Past: Beyond the Dominant Narratives

Unearthing the Ror: A Journey into Sindh's Forgotten Dynasty

Imagine a dynasty shrouded in the mists of time, its story whispered in ancient poetry and etched onto crumbling stones. This is the Ror Dynasty, rulers of Sindh in present-day Pakistan, a kingdom that flourished over 1500 years ago. For centuries, their tale has been a tapestry woven with threads of legend and half-truths. But now, armed with the tools of modern archaeology and a spirit of critical inquiry, we're peeling back the layers of history to reveal a more vibrant and complex picture of this forgotten realm.

Whispers from the Past: Piecing Together the Ror Puzzle

Our journey begins with the echoes of the past. The epic poem "Shah Jo Risalo," a masterpiece of Sindhi literature, sings of the Ror, offering glimpses into their customs and beliefs. Inscriptions on weathered coins and temple walls whisper the names of kings and their conquests. These tantalizing clues are our starting point, but they're just the beginning.

In the ancient city of Alor, once the beating heart of the Ror kingdom, archaeologists are unearthing a treasure trove of artifacts. Imagine delicately painted pottery, shimmering jewelry, and coins bearing the faces of long-dead rulers. These objects bring the Ror to life, allowing us to touch the past and connect with a people who walked this land centuries ago.

Beyond the Legends: Challenging the Traditional Narrative

But history, like a mischievous storyteller, can sometimes play tricks on us. Traditional accounts, often colored by the biases of their authors, may not always tell the whole story. And the archaeological record, though rich in detail, can be frustratingly incomplete. It's like trying to solve a puzzle with missing pieces.

So, we must be detectives, questioning every assumption and seeking out alternative interpretations. Could the Ror, traditionally believed to be of noble Indian origin, have roots in the nomadic Scythian or Parthian cultures? Did their kingdom stretch as far as ancient texts suggest, or was their realm more confined?

A Society in Motion: Unveiling the Ror Way of Life

To truly understand the Ror, we need to delve into the fabric of their society. Imagine a hierarchical world, with the king at its apex, and a complex web of social classes below. What were the lives of ordinary people like? What gods did they worship? Did their beliefs shape their daily routines and interactions?

The Ror were likely farmers, cultivating the fertile lands along the Indus River. But did they also engage in trade, exchanging goods with distant lands? And how did their religious beliefs, a blend of Hinduism and perhaps other faiths, influence their social and economic structures?

Rewriting History: A New Timeline for the Ror

Our quest to understand the Ror is like assembling a giant jigsaw puzzle. Each new discovery, each reinterpretation, brings us closer to the complete picture. By weaving together archaeological evidence, critical analysis of traditional sources, and fresh perspectives, we can create a more accurate and nuanced timeline of their reign.

This revised history will not only enrich our understanding of the past but also inspire future generations. Imagine textbooks filled with vibrant stories of the Ror, documentaries bringing their world to life, and museum exhibits showcasing their exquisite artifacts. By sharing this knowledge, we can ensure that the legacy of the Ror Dynasty, once lost in the shadows, is finally brought into the light.

The Ror Dynasty, a forgotten chapter in the history of South Asia, is waiting to be rediscovered. Join us on this exciting journey as we unearth their secrets and reclaim their place in the grand narrative of human history.

The Soomras: Sindh's Unsung Heroes of Art and Culture

Forget the history books that drone on about conquests and kings! Let's dive into the vibrant world of the Soomras, who ruled Sindh (in modern-day Pakistan) way back in the 11th to 14th centuries. These guys weren't just about politics and power; they were serious patrons of the arts, leaving behind a legacy that still echoes through Sindh today.

Architectural Wonders

Imagine a mosque so grand, it's the largest in all of Sindh! That's the Great Mosque of Thatta, a masterpiece of Islamic architecture built by the last Soomra ruler. Picture intricate brickwork, dazzling tilework, and a prayer hall that will take your breath away.

And don't forget the Makli Necropolis, a sprawling city of the dead where Soomra royalty were laid to rest. It's a melting pot of architectural styles – Islamic domes meet Hindu carvings, all nestled amongst ancient Buddhist stupas. It's like a history lesson etched in stone!

Oh, and have you heard of the Rato Kot Fort? This 11th-century behemoth stands guard over Thatta, offering stunning views of the countryside. Just imagine the Soomra kings gazing out from its ramparts, plotting their next move!

Poetry, Music, and a Touch of Magic

The Soomras were more than just builders; they were poets and musicians too! Jam Nizamuddin II, their last ruler, penned the epic poem "Shah Jo Risalo," a tale of bravery and rebellion against invaders. Think of it as Sindh's own "Game of Thrones," full of drama and intrigue.

And the music! The Soomra era was a golden age for Sindhi tunes. They brought in new instruments, nurtured talented musicians, and basically threw one heck of a party for the senses.

Harmony in a Diverse Land

The Soomras were masters of keeping the peace. Sindh was a melting pot of religions and cultures, but they fostered tolerance and understanding. No religious persecution here! They even championed social reforms, like banning the horrifying practice of sati (where widows were forced to jump into their husband's funeral pyre – yikes!).

Seafaring Sultans of Trade

These guys weren't afraid to set sail! The Soomras built a vast network of trade routes, connecting Sindh with far-flung lands like the Middle East and Africa. Think of them as the ancient world's version of Amazon, bringing exotic goods and spices to Sindh while spreading their own culture far and wide.

Bringing the Past to Life

Want to explore the Soomra world for yourself? We're creating a digital map of all their amazing monuments and archaeological sites! Imagine zooming in on the Great Mosque of Thatta, then hopping over to the Makli Necropolis with a click of your mouse. It's like having a time machine in your pocket!

So, there you have it – the Soomras, Sindh's forgotten heroes of art, culture, and good vibes. Their legacy lives on, waiting to be rediscovered. Now, go forth and explore!

The Samma Resistance: A David vs. Goliath Tale of Resilience and Innovation

Imagine a small kingdom, nestled in the heart of modern-day Pakistan, standing defiant against a relentless tide of empires. This is the story of the Samma dynasty, a people who, against all odds, held their ground against the mighty Mughals, the seafaring Portuguese, and the formidable Persians for over three centuries. This wasn't just about brute force; it was a testament to the power of human resilience, strategic brilliance, and the unwavering spirit of a people determined to protect their homeland.

Guerrilla Warfare: The Art of the Unexpected

Think of the Samma warriors as masters of the element of surprise. They were the ninjas of their time, utilizing the terrain like a chameleon blends into its surroundings. They'd strike swiftly and vanish into the shadows, leaving their enemies bewildered and demoralized. This guerrilla warfare, coupled with cunning ambushes in narrow passes and the strategic use of fortifications, transformed Sindh into a formidable fortress.

More Than Muscle: The Power of Unity

But the Samma resistance was more than just military prowess. It was a symphony of unity, where local communities and tribes joined forces, creating an intricate web of resistance. Imagine villagers sharing whispers of enemy movements, blacksmiths forging weapons, and farmers providing sustenance – a collective heartbeat fueling the fight for freedom. This unity, this shared sense of purpose, was the bedrock of their resilience.

A Legacy Etched in Time

The echoes of the Samma resistance reverberate even today. Their story is a beacon of hope, a testament to the power of courage and strategic thinking in the face of overwhelming adversity. It reminds us that even the smallest among us can rise against giants, leaving an indelible mark on history.

Bringing the Samma Story to Life

This isn't just a tale confined to dusty history books. It's a story that begs to be told, to be experienced. Imagine interactive exhibits where you navigate the treacherous terrain alongside Samma warriors, documentaries that bring their battles to life, and graphic novels that capture the drama and heroism of their struggle. Let's weave this narrative into our educational tapestry, inspiring future generations with the legacy of the Samma resistance.

The Samma resistance is a testament to the indomitable human spirit, a beacon reminding us that even against overwhelming odds, unity, innovation, and unwavering determination can prevail.

Let's ensure their story continues to echo through time, inspiring generations to come.

Hidden Histories: Whispers from the Shadows

"They may erase my name from the scrolls, but they cannot erase my impact from the hearts of my people." - Queen Amanirenas of Kush (allegedly)

History, as we know it, is a tapestry woven with threads of bias. The victors, the powerful, the privileged – their stories are embroidered in bold colors, while the voices of the marginalized fade into the background, their contributions rendered nearly invisible. But what if we could unravel those muted threads, those whispers from the shadows, and bring their stories to life?

This journey takes us beyond the well-trodden paths of emperors and conquerors, to the hidden corners where remarkable individuals defied the odds and shaped their worlds. It's a quest to reclaim the legacies of those history tried to forget.

Unveiling the Unseen:

Imagine a Mongolian princess, Khutulun, thundering across the steppe on horseback, her laughter echoing across the wind. Legend claims she was so skilled in combat that she could defeat any man in her tribe. Did she yearn for love, or did she scoff at the constraints of traditional marriage? What dreams burned within her heart as she galloped towards the horizon?

Travel south to the Kingdom of Kush, where Queen Amanirenas, adorned in gold and ivory, stared down the might of the Roman Empire. Her defiance shook the foundations of their power, yet her name barely graces our history books. What strategies did she employ? What sacrifices did she make to protect her people?

These are just glimpses into the lives of those who dared to lead, to resist, to leave their mark on the world. Their stories, once silenced, are now begging to be heard.

Why These Voices Matter:

   A Fuller Picture: History is not a monolithic narrative. It's a kaleidoscope of experiences, and by including the marginalized, we gain a more complete and nuanced understanding of the past.
   Challenging the Status Quo: Unearthing these hidden histories challenges the dominant narratives that often perpetuate stereotypes and inequalities. It forces us to question who gets to tell the story and whose voices are deemed worthy of remembering.
   Inspiration for the Future: The courage and resilience of these forgotten figures can inspire us to challenge injustice, fight for equality, and create a more inclusive world.

Bringing History to Life:

Imagine a documentary that transports you to ancient Kush, where you stand beside Queen Amanirenas as she rallies her troops against the Roman legions. Or perhaps an interactive website where you can explore the life of Khutulun through animated maps, historical documents, and even a "choose your own adventure" style game that allows you to make decisions that impact her journey.

We can use technology and creativity to:

Weave Compelling Narratives: Employ evocative storytelling, music, and visuals to bring these characters and their eras to life.

Create Immersive Experiences: Utilize virtual reality, augmented reality, and interactive maps to transport audiences to these historical worlds.

Empower Participation: Develop online platforms where users can contribute their own research, stories, and artistic interpretations, creating a living archive of marginalized histories.

A Call to Action:

This is not just about uncovering the past; it's about shaping the future. Let's become history detectives, seeking out the forgotten stories in our own communities. Let's support museums and organizations dedicated to preserving these legacies. Let's use our voices to amplify the whispers from the shadows and ensure that these remarkable individuals are finally given the recognition they deserve.

Partition's Scars: Sindhi Identity in Flux

Mapping the Displaced: A Tapestry of the Sindhi Diaspora

A Journey Through Time and Space

The partition of India in 1947 was a cataclysmic event that reshaped the subcontinent. Amidst the chaos and violence, hundreds of thousands of Sindhi Hindus were uprooted from their ancestral homeland. This diaspora, scattered across the globe, carries with it a rich cultural heritage and a poignant story of resilience.

A Forced Exodus

Imagine the heart-wrenching scene: families fleeing their homes, clutching precious belongings, and casting a final glance at the land they've always known. The Sindhi Hindus, a community deeply rooted in the fertile plains of Sindh, were forced to embark on a perilous journey into the unknown.

A Global Odyssey

The diaspora's footprints can be found on every continent. From the bustling streets of Mumbai to the serene landscapes of Canada, Sindhi communities have flourished, adapting to new cultures while preserving their unique identity.

India: The majority of Sindhi Hindus sought refuge in India, particularly in Maharashtra, Gujarat, and Rajasthan. They established thriving businesses, contributed to the nation's economy, and enriched its cultural tapestry.

United Kingdom: The British Raj left an enduring legacy on India, and many Sindhi Hindus migrated to the UK. They excelled in various fields, from medicine and engineering to finance and arts.

United States, Canada, and Australia: These nations welcomed Sindhi immigrants with open arms. They have made significant contributions to their adopted countries, particularly in fields like technology, healthcare, and education.

East Africa: A smaller but vibrant Sindhi community settled in countries like Kenya, Tanzania, and Uganda. They played a crucial role in the region's economic development.

A Tapestry of Experiences

The experiences of Sindhi migrants have been as diverse as the countries they settled in. Some faced discrimination and prejudice, while others were welcomed with open arms. Despite the challenges, they persevered, building new lives and forging strong bonds with their fellow Sindhis.

Preserving the Legacy

To ensure that the rich heritage of the Sindhi diaspora is not lost to time, numerous initiatives have been undertaken:

Cultural Organizations: Organizations like the Sindhi Foundation and the Sindhi Association of North America work tirelessly to promote Sindhi language, literature, and music.
Community Events: Annual festivals and gatherings bring Sindhis together, fostering a sense of belonging and identity.
Online Platforms: Social media and online forums have emerged as powerful tools for connecting with fellow Sindhis worldwide.

An Interactive Map: A Visual Journey

To truly appreciate the global reach of the Sindhi diaspora, an interactive online map can be a powerful tool. This virtual journey would allow users to:

Explore the diaspora's footprint: Pinpoint the locations of major Sindhi communities around the world.

Discover personal stories: Listen to firsthand accounts of migration, settlement, and cultural preservation.

Engage with virtual exhibits: View historical documents, photographs, and artifacts that tell the story of the Sindhi diaspora.

Connect with fellow Sindhis: Join online forums and social media groups to share experiences and build relationships.

By combining historical research, personal narratives, and cutting-edge technology, this interactive map can bring the Sindhi diaspora to life, inspiring future generations to carry forward their rich legacy.

Subtopic 2: Language as Lifeline: Keeping Sindhi Alive

Imagine a vibrant tapestry, woven with threads of history, stories, and songs. This tapestry is the Sindhi language, a rich inheritance carried across oceans and continents by its people. But in the bustling marketplaces and quiet suburbs of their new homes, the threads begin to fray. Children, immersed in the melodies of their adopted lands, sometimes struggle to recall the lullabies sung in their mother tongue. This is the challenge facing Sindhi in diaspora – a fight against fading voices and forgotten whispers.

It's a story echoed in communities around the world. As Sindhi families build new lives, the everyday symphony of their language can be drowned out by the dominant soundscape. Schoolyards ring with unfamiliar tongues, television screens flicker with foreign faces, and the whispers of Sindhi become less frequent, a precious heirloom tucked away in the attic of memory.

But hope is not lost. Think of dedicated teachers, passionate like gardeners, tending to the seeds of language in vibrant Sindhi schools. Picture community centers transformed into bustling "bazaars" of conversation, where elders share folktales and laughter mingles with the aroma of chai. And envision the digital world ablaze with Sindhi blogs, online forums buzzing with discussions, and social media groups echoing with the music of the language.

These are the lifelines, the threads that weave the tapestry anew. They are the tools that empower a new generation to claim their heritage, to sing the songs of their ancestors, and to paint their dreams in the colors of Sindhi.

More Than Words: Why Sindhi Matters

Language is more than just a tool for communication; it's the very soul of a culture. Embedded within its words are the values, the history, the very essence of a people. To lose Sindhi is to risk losing a part of oneself, a severance from the roots that nourish identity.

Imagine a young Sindhi girl, growing up in London. By speaking Sindhi, she unlocks a treasure chest of stories from her grandparents, stories that whisper of the Indus River, of ancient traditions, and of a homeland she may have never seen. Through language, she connects with her heritage, building a bridge between her present and her past.

Building Bridges: A 21st Century Approach to Language Learning

To truly revitalize Sindhi, we need to embrace innovation and creativity. Imagine a language curriculum that leaps off the textbook page and comes alive!

Interactive Apps: Learning Sindhi through gamified apps that make grammar fun and vocabulary stick.

Learn Sindhi. Speak Sindhi. St - Apps on Google Play

Virtual Reality: Immersing students in a vibrant, virtual Sindh, where they can practice conversations in a bustling marketplace or a traditional village.
Cultural Exchanges: Connecting diaspora communities with Sindhi speakers in Sindh through online platforms, fostering friendships and language partnerships.

By weaving technology and cultural immersion into the learning experience, we can make Sindhi relevant and engaging for a new generation.

A Global Tapestry: The Sindhi Language Foundation

Organizations like the Sindhi Language Foundation are beacons of hope, championing the language and fostering a sense of community. Their online platform is a digital "diwan," a gathering place where learners of all ages can access a wealth of resources. Imagine interactive lessons that bring the language to life, cultural activities that celebrate Sindhi traditions, and a vibrant online community that connects Sindhi speakers across the globe.

The revitalization of Sindhi is a collective effort, a symphony played by teachers, community leaders, technology innovators, and, most importantly, by families determined to keep their heritage alive. It's a testament to the enduring power of language, a lifeline connecting generations and ensuring that the tapestry of Sindhi culture continues to weave its magic across the world.

Subtopic 3: Negotiating Identity: Hybridity and Belonging

Imagine a Sindhi family gathered around a dinner table in London. The aroma of spicy biryani fills the air, but alongside it, the clatter of forks instead of hands. This is a snapshot of the Sindhi diaspora – a people scattered across the globe, carrying within them the echoes of the Indus River, while navigating the bustling streets of London, New York, or Toronto. Their journey is one of constant negotiation, a delicate dance between holding onto ancestral memories and embracing the vibrant pulse of their new homes.

1. More Than Just a Label

"Identity" isn't just a word in a textbook for the Sindhi diaspora. It's a living, breathing thing, shaped by the whispers of their ancestors, the trauma of displacement, and the exhilarating possibilities of new beginnings. They are the inheritors of a rich cultural tapestry woven with threads of Sufism, the poetry of Shah Abdul Latif Bhittai, and the vibrant colors of Ajrak. Yet, they are also forging new identities, infused with the flavors and rhythms of their adopted lands.

2. A Tapestry of Influences

Hybridity isn't a compromise; it's a source of strength. Think of a young Sindhi woman in Toronto, effortlessly switching between Sindhi and English, her wardrobe a fusion of traditional shalwar kameez and modern Western styles. Or picture a Sindhi musician in New York, blending the soulful strains of the alghoza flute with jazz rhythms, creating a sound that is both ancient and utterly contemporary. This is how culture evolves – it breathes, it adapts, it finds new expressions.

3. Longing for the Lost Homeland

The concept of "home" for the Sindhi diaspora is bittersweet. It's the scent of roasted chickpeas on the streets of Hyderabad, Pakistan, a memory etched in their hearts. It's the stories their grandparents tell of a land left behind, a land that lives on in their dreams. But "home" is also the community they've built in their new country, the friends who become family, the places where they feel a sense of belonging. It's a constant search for that elusive feeling of rootedness, a place where their hearts can truly rest.

4. Giving Voice to the Diaspora

Imagine sitting down with an elderly Sindhi woman in London, her eyes sparkling as she recounts her family's journey from Sindh to India during Partition. Or listening to a young Sindhi-Canadian artist describe how they express their cultural heritage through their paintings. Ethnographic research and oral history projects are not just academic exercises; they are acts of preserving these precious stories, ensuring that the voices of the Sindhi diaspora are heard and their experiences honored.

5. A Continuing Story

The Sindhi diaspora is a testament to the resilience of the human spirit. Their story is one of adaptation, reinvention, and the enduring power of culture. It's a story that continues to unfold, with each generation adding their own unique verse to the rich tapestry of Sindhi identity.

To further enhance this section, consider incorporating:

Personal anecdotes: Weave in real-life stories of individuals from the Sindhi diaspora.
Sensory details: Use vivid language to evoke the sights, sounds, smells, and tastes of Sindhi culture.
Visual elements: Include images or links to videos that showcase the diversity of the Sindhi diaspora.
Interactive elements: Pose questions to the reader, encouraging them to reflect on their own experiences of identity and belonging.

By making the content more personal, relatable, and engaging, you can truly bring the story of the Sindhi diaspora to life.

A Fractured Tapestry: The Sindhi Experience of Partition

A Personal Journey Through History

The Partition of India in 1947 was a cataclysmic event that reshaped the subcontinent. It was a time of immense suffering, displacement, and violence. Yet, within this chaos, countless individual stories emerged, each a testament to the human spirit's resilience. The Sindhi community, a vibrant and culturally rich people, were deeply impacted by this upheaval. Their experiences, often overlooked, offer a unique perspective on the Partition's far-reaching consequences.

A Homeland Lost

Sindh, a fertile land nestled between the Indus River and the Thar Desert, was once a thriving hub of culture and commerce. It was home to Hindus, Muslims, and Sikhs who lived in harmony for centuries. However, the political winds of the time swept through Sindh, tearing apart its social fabric. The newly drawn borders split families and communities, leaving behind a trail of broken dreams and shattered lives.

A Journey of Displacement

For many Sindhis, the Partition was a forced migration. They were uprooted from their ancestral homes, leaving behind cherished memories and material possessions. The journey to their new homeland was fraught with danger and uncertainty. Trains, the primary mode of transport, were overcrowded and often targeted by mobs. Many Sindhis lost their loved ones during this perilous journey.

Rebuilding Lives in a New Land

Those who survived the ordeal found themselves in a strange and unfamiliar land. They had to rebuild their lives from scratch, often facing discrimination and prejudice. Despite these challenges, the Sindhi community displayed remarkable resilience. They established new homes, businesses, and cultural institutions, preserving their heritage and traditions.

A Digital Archive: Preserving the Past

To honor the sacrifices of our ancestors and to ensure that their stories are never forgotten, we must create a digital archive of Sindhi Partition narratives. This digital repository will serve as a testament to the resilience and courage of the Sindhi people. It will allow future generations to connect with their roots and learn from the mistakes of the past.

A Call to Action

I urge you to join us in this endeavor. Share your family's stories, donate photographs, and help us build a comprehensive digital archive. By preserving our history, we can inspire future generations to work towards a more just and equitable world. Let us honor the sacrifices of our ancestors by building a brighter future for our children.

Whispers of Wisdom: Sindhi Folktales and their Enduring Relevance

Unraveling the Archetypes: Recurring Motifs and their Significance in Sindhi Folktales

Sindhi folklore is a vibrant tapestry woven with threads of ancient stories, legends, and fables. Passed down through countless generations, these tales are not merely entertainment; they are vessels carrying the very essence of Sindhi culture, values, and beliefs.

One of the most captivating aspects of Sindhi folktales is the recurrence of specific motifs and archetypes. These recurring elements act as symbolic threads, connecting the stories and offering a glimpse into the heart of Sindhi society.

Identifying and Analyzing Recurring Motifs and Archetypes

Let's delve into some of the prominent motifs and archetypes found in Sindhi folktales:

The Trickster Figure: A ubiquitous archetype across cultures, the trickster in Sindhi folklore is often a cunning and mischievous character who relies on wit and intelligence to outsmart others. Umaro, a clever and resourceful peasant, is a prime example of this archetype.
The Wise Woman: A recurring figure of wisdom and guidance, often depicted as an elderly woman with a profound understanding of life. Moriro, a revered prophetess, exemplifies this archetype in Sindhi folklore.
The Magical Creature: Sindhi folktales are populated with an array of magical creatures, both benevolent and malevolent, that play pivotal roles in the narratives. Fairies, demons, and jinn are just a few examples.

The Hero's Journey: A common narrative structure, the hero's journey in Sindhi folktales typically involves a protagonist who must overcome a series of challenges and trials to achieve their goal. The story of Umar Marvi is a classic example.

The Love Story: Love, loss, and sacrifice are central themes in many Sindhi folktales, often highlighting the enduring power of love. The tale of Sassi and Punnu is a poignant example of this enduring theme.

Exploring Symbolic Meanings and Cultural Connections

The motifs and archetypes in Sindhi folktales are not mere literary devices; they are imbued with deep symbolic meanings that reflect the cultural values and beliefs of the Sindhi people.

The trickster figure, like Umaro, embodies resilience and resourcefulness, traits valued in Sindhi society.

The wise woman, such as Moriro, represents the wisdom and knowledge of elders, highlighting the importance of respecting and learning from them.

Magical creatures symbolize the supernatural forces believed to be at play in the world, reflecting the spiritual aspects of Sindhi culture.

The hero's journey serves as a metaphor for life's challenges and the importance of perseverance.

Love stories emphasize the power of love to transcend obstacles, a value cherished in Sindhi society.

Comparing Sindhi Folktale Motifs with Other Cultures

While the motifs and archetypes in Sindhi folktales share similarities with those found in other cultures, they also possess unique characteristics. For instance, the Sindhi trickster is often more mischievous and cunning, while the wise woman holds greater power and influence.

Comparing these elements across cultures allows us to appreciate both the universal themes that connect us and the unique cultural nuances that make each culture distinct.

Practical Application: A Database for Researchers and Educators

To enhance accessibility and facilitate research, a comprehensive database of Sindhi folktales, categorized by motifs and themes, could be developed. This valuable resource would benefit scholars, educators, and anyone interested in exploring Sindhi folklore.

The database could include:

Title and author/storyteller information
Themes and motifs
Links to audio recordings or videos
Translations into various languages

Conclusion

Sindhi folktales are a treasure trove of cultural insights, offering a window into the values, beliefs, and traditions of the Sindhi people. By unraveling the recurring motifs and archetypes, we gain a deeper understanding of the human experience and the universal themes that resonate across cultures.

This exploration not only enriches our appreciation of Sindhi folklore but also fosters cross-cultural understanding and appreciation.

Mirrors of Society: Reflecting Social Norms and Values in Sindhi Folktales

Sindhi folktales, like the intricate threads of a precious Ajrak, weave together stories that reveal the heart and soul of the Sindhi people. These tales are not merely fanciful narratives, but vibrant reflections of the social norms, gender roles, and power dynamics that have shaped Sindhi society for centuries.

A Tapestry of Values

Imagine sitting around a crackling fire on a cool desert night, listening to the elders recount tales of bravery, love, and sacrifice. These stories, passed down through generations, instill the core values of Sindhi culture. Tales like "Mumal and Rano" celebrate the unbreakable bond of sisterhood and the importance of family loyalty, while the story of "Umar Marui" echoes with the spirit of resilience and courage in the face of adversity. These narratives serve as moral compasses, guiding the community towards ideals of honor, hospitality, and respect.

Gender Roles: A Dance of Tradition and Change

Sindhi folktales often portray traditional gender roles, with men as protectors and providers, and women as nurturers and homemakers. Yet, amidst these familiar patterns, emerge powerful female figures who defy expectations. Sassi, from the epic love story "Sassi and Punnu," challenges societal constraints in her pursuit of love, while Rani Hinglaj, the warrior goddess, embodies strength and independence. These stories offer a glimpse into the complex and evolving roles of women in Sindhi society.

Power Dynamics: Echoes of Authority and Resistance

The tales also reflect the power dynamics inherent in any society. Kings and queens, with their majestic courts and decrees, represent authority and control. However, Sindhi folklore also gives voice to the common people, their struggles, and their resistance to injustice. Tales like "Uthman Ghani" satirize the hypocrisy of those in power, while "Umar Marui" critiques oppression and champions the fight for freedom. These narratives remind us that even in the face of power, the human spirit yearns for justice and equality.

Folktales as Seeds of Change

Sindhi folktales are not merely relics of the past; they are living narratives that continue to inspire and challenge. By exploring these stories, we can spark critical thinking and dialogue about social issues that resonate even today. In classrooms and community gatherings, these tales can serve as powerful tools for exploring themes of gender equality, social justice, and the importance of cultural heritage.

The Enduring Legacy of Sindhi Folktales

Like the shimmering sands of the Thar Desert, Sindhi folktales hold within them the essence of a rich and vibrant culture. They are mirrors reflecting the values, struggles, and aspirations of the Sindhi people. By listening to these stories, we embark on a journey of understanding, not just of a particular culture, but of the universal human experience.

Let's dive into the magical world of Sindhi folktales and discover how these age-old stories can spark a love for learning and guide young hearts towards a life filled with kindness, courage, and wisdom!

Imagine a crackling campfire under a desert sky, stars twinkling like diamonds above. A wise elder, with eyes that hold the wisdom of generations, begins to weave a tale...

This is how Sindhi folktales have been passed down for centuries, carrying with them precious lessons that still resonate today. These stories aren't just entertainment; they're a secret codebook for life, teaching children about honesty, compassion, and the strength to overcome any obstacle.

Unlocking the Secrets of Sindhi Folktales

Honesty is a superpower! Remember the story of "Momal Rano," where the beautiful Momal chooses a simple life with her true love, Rana, over the riches offered by the deceitful Sorath? Her honesty, like a shining beacon, guides her to true happiness. In a world where "fake news" and little white lies can be tempting, Momal's story reminds us that truthfulness is always the most powerful weapon.

Kindness is like a ripple in a pond. In the tale of "Lila Chanesar," Lila, a poor woodcutter's daughter, shows compassion to a lost and injured prince. Her kindness not only heals the prince but also transforms her own life. Just like Lila, we can create ripples of positive change in the world by showing empathy and helping those in need, whether it's a classmate who's being bullied or a stranger who needs a helping hand.

Greed is a monster that devours happiness. The story of the greedy merchant in "The Seven Wise Masters" warns us that chasing wealth and possessions can lead to a lonely and empty life. This tale reminds us to appreciate the simple joys in life, like spending time with loved ones and appreciating the beauty of nature, instead of always wanting more.

Never give up, even when the path is thorny! Think of Sassui, the devoted heroine of "Sassui Punhun," who braves scorching deserts and treacherous mountains in her unwavering pursuit of her beloved Punhun. Her story echoes the spirit of Malala Yousafzai, who faced incredible danger to fight for education. Both remind us that with determination and resilience, we can achieve our dreams and make a difference in the world.

Be a hero, even when you're afraid! The legendary Marui, from the tale of "Umar Marui," defied a powerful king to defend her freedom. Her courage inspires us to stand up for what is right, even when it's difficult. Whether it's speaking out against injustice or simply standing up to a bully, we can all be heroes in our own way.

Bringing the Stories to Life: Interactive Workshops

Imagine a workshop where children don't just listen to stories, but become part of them!

Step into the story: Children can dress up as their favorite characters, create puppets, and act out scenes from the folktales. Imagine a room filled with little Momals, Ranas, and Lilas, bringing these ancient stories to life!

Modern-day magic: Let's reimagine these tales in a modern context! What if Momal was a social media influencer facing pressure to promote a product she doesn't believe in? Or if Lila was a young girl who starts a campaign to help refugees? By adapting the stories to their own lives, children can see how these timeless values are still relevant today.

Create your own moral compass: Using art supplies, children can design a colorful compass with each point representing a value from the folktales – honesty, kindness, courage, and perseverance. This becomes a personal guide to help them navigate the challenges of life.

Storytelling circles: Encourage children to share their own family stories and traditions, creating a tapestry of voices and experiences. Grandparents can be invited to share their wisdom, making the workshops a truly intergenerational experience.

Let's ignite the imaginations of young minds and empower them to become the heroes of their own stories!

By weaving together the magic of Sindhi folktales with creative activities and modern-day connections, we can create a learning experience that is both enriching and unforgettable. These stories, passed down through generations, hold the key to unlocking a world of wisdom, compassion, and courage within each child.

A Modern Reimagining of "Sohni Mehar"

The Premise:

In a bustling metropolis, where tradition and modernity collide, Sohni, a young, aspiring artist, and Mehar, a tech entrepreneur, find themselves drawn to each other. Their love story is a modern retelling of the classic Sindhi folktale, "Sohni Mehar," where societal expectations and technological advancements challenge the course of true love.

Sohni: A passionate, independent artist, Sohni defies societal norms to pursue her dreams. She's not just a damsel in distress, but a strong, complex woman who yearns for freedom and self-expression.

Mehar: A brilliant, yet reserved tech entrepreneur, Mehar is torn between his love for Sohni and his family's expectations. He's a man of science and reason, struggling to reconcile his logical mind with his emotional heart.

A Modern Twist:

The Digital Divide: Sohni and Mehar's love story is complicated by the digital divide between their worlds. While Mehar is immersed in the virtual realm of technology, Sohni finds solace in the tangible world of art.

Societal Expectations: Both Sohni and Mehar face pressure from their families to conform to traditional roles. Sohni's parents want her to marry a wealthy businessman, while Mehar's family expects him to focus on his career and settle down with a suitable bride.

A Risky Encounter: Instead of a river, the couple's love is tested by a dangerous cyber threat. A rival tech company, jealous of Mehar's success, launches a cyberattack that could destroy his business and endanger their relationship.

Interactive Storytelling:

Readers can influence the story's outcome through choices:

The Secret Meeting: Will Sohni and Mehar risk a secret meeting, knowing the consequences?

The Cyberattack: How will they protect their love and their business from the cyber threat?

The Ultimate Sacrifice: Will Sohni and Mehar choose love over duty, or will they sacrifice their happiness for the sake of their families?

Visual and Audio Elements:

Animated Short Films: Create short animated films that depict key scenes from the story, using a blend of traditional and modern animation techniques.

Interactive Music Videos: Develop interactive music videos where viewers can choose different camera angles and storylines.

Virtual Reality Experience: Immerse the audience in the world of Sohni and Mehar through a VR experience. They can explore virtual spaces, interact with characters, and make choices that affect the narrative.

By combining these elements, we can create a captivating and immersive experience that honors the spirit of the original folktale while resonating with a modern audience.

The Rhythm of Sindh: Music and Dance as Cultural Expressions

Sufi Music in Sindh: A Journey Through the Soul of the Land

The air hangs heavy with the scent of jasmine and incense as the sun dips below the horizon, casting long shadows across the ancient land of Sindh. A hush falls over the crowd gathered in the courtyard of a dargah, a Sufi shrine. Then, a lone voice rises, plaintive and yearning, accompanied by the rhythmic beat of a dholak drum. This is the sound of Sufi music in Sindh, a music that speaks to the soul and carries with it centuries of tradition and devotion.

A Tapestry of Melodies and Mysticism

Sufi music in Sindh is more than just a collection of songs; it's a journey into the heart of a rich and vibrant culture. Imagine the mournful strains of a kafi, a narrative poem that unfolds like a tapestry of love, loss, and longing. Picture the ecstatic energy of a kalama, a lyrical outpouring of joy and devotion that sets hearts ablaze. And feel the hypnotic rhythm of a ghosia, a Sufi chant that transports listeners to a state of spiritual ecstasy.

The Pioneers of Sufi Music in Sindh

This musical tradition owes much to the Sufi saints and mystics who have graced the land of Sindh over the centuries. Shah Abdul Latif Bhittai, the revered poet and musician, stands tall among them. His verses, infused with profound spiritual insights, continue to resonate with people from all walks of life. Sachal Sarmast, another luminary, poured his soul into his poetry and music, leaving behind a legacy of passion and social commentary.

Instruments of the Soul

The music of Sindh is brought to life by a variety of instruments, each with its own unique voice. The dholak, a double-headed drum, provides the rhythmic backbone, while the tamburo, a long-necked lute, adds a melodic layer. The sarangi, a bowed string instrument, weaves in soulful melodies that tug at the heartstrings.

Lyrical Journeys into the Divine

The lyrics of Sindhi Sufi music are steeped in Sufi philosophy, exploring themes of love, devotion, and the unity of all beings. The concept of Wahdat al-Wujud, the oneness of existence, finds expression in metaphors and allegories that invite listeners to contemplate the divine essence within themselves and all of creation.

A Beacon of Harmony and Hope

Sufi music has long served as a bridge between communities in Sindh, transcending differences of religion, ethnicity, and social class. It has the power to unite people in shared moments of spiritual devotion and cultural celebration. In a world often divided by conflict and misunderstanding, Sufi music offers a message of peace, tolerance, and hope.

Contemporary Echoes of Tradition

Today, Sufi music in Sindh continues to thrive, adapting to new contexts while remaining deeply rooted in its rich heritage. Sufi musicians are using their voices to address contemporary issues, from social injustice to environmental concerns. They are also carrying the torch of tradition forward, ensuring that the soulful melodies and profound messages of Sufi music continue to inspire and uplift generations to come.

Conclusion

Sufi music in Sindh is a testament to the enduring power of music to touch the human spirit. It is a journey through the soul of a land, a celebration of love, devotion, and the search for the divine. As the strains of Sufi music echo across the centuries, they carry with them a message of hope and unity, reminding us of the shared humanity that binds us all.

Instruments of Tradition: Where the Soul of Sindh Sings

Imagine the haunting wail of a flute echoing across the desert sands, the rhythmic pulse of drums urging dancers into a frenzy, and the delicate melody of a stringed instrument weaving tales of love and loss. This is the magic of Sindhi music, a vibrant tapestry woven with the threads of history, culture, and the unique voices of its traditional instruments.

Forget dry museum displays! Let's embark on a journey where each instrument comes alive. We'll feel the smooth, worn wood of an Alghoza, a double flute that seems to breathe the very essence of the Sindhi landscape. Picture a shepherd playing a mournful tune on his Borrindo, a single-reed instrument that pours out the sorrows and joys of a nomadic life. And who can resist the infectious energy of the Dhol, the mighty drum that sets hearts racing at weddings and festivals?

But these instruments are more than just objects; they are vessels of heritage, lovingly crafted by skilled artisans who have inherited generations of knowledge. Imagine the calloused hands of a master craftsman shaping a Surando, a bowed instrument that sings with the voice of the Sindhi people. See the meticulous care with which he selects the wood, feeling its grain, listening for its inner resonance. This is an art form passed down through families, where secrets whispered from father to son ensure that each instrument carries the soul of Sindh.

And what about the Khartal, those simple wooden clappers that create intricate rhythms in the hands of a skilled musician? Or the Dilo, a large earthenware pot that resonates with a deep, earthy sound, connecting the music to the very soil of Sindh? Even the shimmering Manjiras, tiny cymbals that accentuate the music with their delicate chime, hold a special place in the hearts of the Sindhi people.

These instruments aren't confined to dusty shelves; they are living, breathing parts of Sindhi culture. They accompany Sufi mystics lost in trance, they provide the soundtrack to joyous celebrations, and they whisper ancient stories around campfires. Each note played is a link to the past, a testament to the resilience and creativity of the Sindhi people.

But tradition doesn't mean stagnation. Master craftsmen are constantly innovating, experimenting with new materials and techniques while staying true to the essence of their craft. They are the guardians of Sindhi musical heritage, ensuring that these instruments continue to resonate in a rapidly changing world.

Now, let's bring this heritage to life in the digital age! Imagine a virtual museum where you can not only see these instruments in intricate detail but also hear their voices. Interactive exhibits, 3D models, and captivating videos will transport you to the heart of Sindh, where you can witness master musicians weaving their magic. This digital space will be a vibrant hub for learning, sharing, and celebrating the rich tapestry of Sindhi music, ensuring that its soul continues to sing for generations to come.

Sindhi Dance: A Tapestry Woven in Time and Rhythm

Imagine a land where the desert wind whispers stories and the Indus River flows with the rhythm of life. This is Sindh, and its soul finds expression in the vibrant tapestry of its dances. Forget dry historical accounts, let's embark on a journey through time and emotion!

1. Echoes of the Past: The Dance of Evolution

Imagine our ancestors, gathered around flickering firelight, their bodies swaying to the rhythm of drums, invoking ancient gods and celebrating the cycles of nature. These primal movements were the seeds from which Sindhi dance blossomed.

Bhagat: Picture a swirling kaleidoscope of color and energy, where dancers become storytellers, embodying gods and heroes with every passionate gesture. Bhagat is a living testament to the power of faith and the enduring connection between the human and the divine.

Chhej: Feel the ground thrum with the powerful footwork of men, their sticks clacking like a vibrant heartbeat. Chhej is a celebration of masculine energy, a joyous dance of camaraderie and celebration, often performed at weddings, where the air crackles with excitement and anticipation.

1. Folk dances of Sindh

Jhumar: Envision a group of women, their movements graceful as the swaying reeds, their faces reflecting the joy and sorrow of life. Jhumar is a dance of the soul, an expression of feminine grace and resilience.

And let's not forget the hypnotic whirl of Dhamaal, a Sufi dance that transports both performer and viewer to a state of spiritual ecstasy, or the enchanting storytelling of Latifani, where women weave narratives with their bodies and voices.

2. More Than Just Steps: Deciphering the Language of Dance

Sindhi dance is a language in itself, a symphony of movement, costume, and symbolism.

Movement: Every gesture, every step, tells a story. The fluid grace of Jhumar speaks of the flowing river, while the energetic jumps of Chhej echo the vibrant pulse of life.

Costume: The dancers are adorned in a riot of colors, each garment a work of art. Sparkling sequins and intricate embroidery catch the light, transforming the performers into living jewels.

Symbolism: Each dance carries a deeper meaning. The circular formations often seen in Sindhi dances symbolize the cyclical nature of life, while the use of specific hand gestures can convey complex emotions or spiritual concepts.

3. Dance as a Lifeline: Connecting Communities and Souls

In Sindh, dance is not merely entertainment; it's the lifeblood that courses through the veins of the community. It's there at weddings, where joyous celebrations erupt in a whirlwind of swirling skirts and rhythmic clapping. It's present in religious ceremonies, where devotion finds expression in every step and gesture. And it's an integral part of festivals, where the whole community comes alive with shared rhythm and movement.

But beyond the social and cultural significance, Sindhi dance offers something more profound. It's a source of healing, a way to connect with one's inner self, and a means of finding solace and strength in the face of life's challenges.

4. A Cinematic Ode: Bringing Sindhi Dance to the World

Imagine a documentary that captures the essence of Sindhi dance, not as a museum exhibit, but as a living, breathing art form. A film that transports viewers to the heart of Sindh, where they can witness the passion, the joy, and the spiritual depth of these dances.

We'll hear the stories of the dancers, the musicians, and the keepers of tradition. We'll see the dances come alive against the backdrop of stunning landscapes, from the rolling sand dunes of the Thar Desert to the bustling streets of Karachi. This film will be a celebration of Sindhi culture, a testament to the power of dance to connect us to our past, our present, and our future.

Conclusion: Keeping the Flame Alive

Sindhi dance is a precious heritage, a gift passed down through generations. It's a testament to the resilience and creativity of the Sindhi people, a reflection of their deep connection to their land and their spirituality. By embracing and celebrating these dances, we ensure that their magic continues to inspire and uplift for generations to come.

Subtopic 4: Fusion and Innovation: Modern Interpretations of Sindhi Music and Dance

Introduction

Imagine a vibrant tapestry woven with threads of ancient melodies and modern rhythms, where traditional dance steps intertwine with contemporary moves. This is the world of modern Sindhi music and dance, a dynamic landscape where tradition meets innovation.

Sindhi music and dance, with roots stretching back millennia, are experiencing a renaissance. Globalization and modern trends have breathed new life into these art forms, leading to exciting fusion styles and contemporary interpretations. Technology has also played a pivotal role, amplifying the voices of Sindhi artists and sharing their creativity with the world.

This exploration delves into the fascinating interplay of tradition and modernity, examining how globalization and technology have shaped Sindhi music and dance, and highlighting the potential for collaboration to further ignite innovation and cultural exchange.

Globalization and Modern Trends: A Cultural Confluence

Globalization has opened a world of possibilities for Sindhi music and dance. It's like a cultural bridge connecting Sindh with the rest of the world, allowing for an exchange of ideas and influences. This has given rise to new musical and dance styles that blend traditional elements with contemporary flavors.

Imagine Sindhi musicians incorporating Western instruments like the electric guitar or saxophone into their compositions, or DJs adding electronic beats to traditional folk songs. Picture Sindhi dancers infusing their performances with elements of hip-hop, jazz, or contemporary dance, creating a mesmerizing fusion of movement and expression.

Globalization has not only led to the creation of new styles but has also amplified the reach of Sindhi music and dance. Thanks to the internet and social media, these art forms are now accessible to a global audience. YouTube, Instagram, and Facebook have become virtual stages where Sindhi artists can share their work with the world, connecting with fans and fellow artists across continents.

Fusion Styles: Where Tradition Meets Innovation

Fusion styles represent the exciting intersection of tradition and modernity. These styles are like a musical melting pot, blending the rich flavors of Sindhi folk music with contemporary sounds and rhythms.

One example is the iconic Pakistani band Junoon, which fuses traditional Sindhi music with Western rock and pop, creating a sound that resonates with audiences across generations. Another example is the innovative dancer Nirmala Lakhani, who seamlessly blends traditional Sindhi dance with contemporary styles like hip hop and jazz, pushing the boundaries of artistic expression.

These fusion styles are often pioneered by young artists who are passionate about their cultural heritage while also embracing new and innovative forms of expression. They are the bridge builders, connecting the past and the present through their artistry.

Contemporary Interpretations of Traditional Forms: Breathing New Life into Tradition

Alongside the emergence of fusion styles, there's a growing movement to reinterpret traditional Sindhi music and dance in new and exciting ways. It's like taking a classic masterpiece and adding a modern twist, making it relevant and appealing to contemporary audiences.

Imagine the legendary singer Abida Parveen, known for her soulful renditions of traditional Sindhi songs, incorporating Western musical arrangements and stage lighting into her performances. Or visualize the renowned dancer Kiran Mansharamani, a master of traditional Sindhi dance, adding contemporary dance techniques and movement styles to her choreography.

These contemporary interpretations not only breathe new life into traditional forms but also make them more accessible to younger generations who are more familiar with contemporary music and dance styles. This ensures that Sindhi music and dance remain vibrant and relevant in the modern world.

The Role of Technology: Amplifying Sindhi Voices

Technology has become an indispensable tool in promoting and disseminating Sindhi music and dance globally. It's like a megaphone amplifying the voices of Sindhi artists and sharing their creativity with the world.

The internet and social media have revolutionized how people access and share cultural content. YouTube, Instagram, and Facebook have become virtual platforms where Sindhi artists can showcase their talent to a global audience, connecting with fans and fellow artists from all corners of the world.

Technology has also enabled the creation of innovative ways to present Sindhi music and dance. The Sindhi Cultural Heritage Project, for example, has developed online resources like videos and audio recordings that document and preserve these art forms, making them accessible to anyone with an internet connection.

Collaboration: A Catalyst for Innovation

One of the most exciting prospects for the future of Sindhi music and dance is the collaboration between traditional artists and contemporary musicians and dancers. This is where the magic happens, where tradition and innovation collide to create something truly unique and inspiring.

Imagine a traditional Sindhi folk singer collaborating with a contemporary music producer to create a new sound that blends ancient melodies with modern beats. Or envision a traditional Sindhi dancer working with a contemporary choreographer to create a performance that fuses traditional steps with modern movements.

These collaborations not only lead to the creation of new and exciting works but also foster a deeper understanding and appreciation of Sindhi music and dance. They bridge the gap between generations, ensuring that these art forms continue to thrive and evolve.

Practical Application: Building a Platform for Collaboration

To facilitate collaboration between traditional artists and contemporary musicians and dancers, we can create a dedicated platform, either online or offline, where they can connect, share ideas, and collaborate on projects. This platform could be a website, a social media group, or even a physical space where artists can meet and work together.

The platform could also serve as an educational resource, providing information about Sindhi music and dance through blog posts, videos, and other materials. It could also be a space where people can share their own experiences and knowledge, fostering a sense of community and cultural exchange.

Conclusion: A Vibrant Future

Sindhi music and dance are at a fascinating crossroads, where tradition and innovation intertwine to create a vibrant and dynamic landscape. Globalization, modern trends, and technology have all played a role in shaping this landscape, leading to the emergence of new styles, contemporary interpretations, and a global reach.

Collaboration between traditional artists and contemporary musicians and dancers holds immense potential for further innovation and cultural exchange. By fostering these collaborations and creating platforms for connection, we can ensure that Sindhi music and dance continue to thrive and inspire for generations to come.

A Culinary Journey: Sindhi Cuisine as a Tapestry of Flavors

A Flavorful Journey Through Sindhi Cuisine

A Culinary Tapestry Woven with Tradition

Sindhi cuisine is a vibrant tapestry, woven with threads of history, tradition, and a generous sprinkling of aromatic spices. It's a cuisine that celebrates simplicity, yet revels in bold flavors. Let's embark on a culinary journey through this delightful cuisine, exploring its staple foods and unique cooking practices.

The Building Blocks of Sindhi Flavor

Wheat Wonders: From soft, pillowy phulkas to crispy, flaky puris, wheat is the cornerstone of Sindhi breadbasket. I still remember the aroma of freshly baked roti wafting through our kitchen, a comforting scent that signaled a hearty meal.

A Grain of Rice, A World of Flavor: Rice, especially basmati, is a staple in Sindhi households. It's the canvas for the colorful and aromatic Sindhi biryani, a dish that's a feast for the senses.

The Humble Pulse, A Protein Powerhouse: Lentils, or daal, are a dietary staple, often simmered to perfection with a medley of spices. They're a comforting and nutritious addition to any meal.

A Garden of Goodness: Fresh, seasonal vegetables like spinach, okra, eggplant, and potatoes are the stars of many Sindhi dishes. I particularly love the way they're transformed into flavorful curries and stir-fries.

From the Sea to the Plate: Seafood, especially fish, is a delicacy in coastal Sindhi regions. It's often grilled, fried, or cooked in aromatic curries.

A Dairy Delight: Milk, yogurt, and ghee add richness and creaminess to many Sindhi dishes. Dahi, a thick, creamy yogurt, is a popular accompaniment to meals.

A Spice Odyssey: Sindhi cuisine is a symphony of spices. Cumin, coriander, turmeric, chili powder, and garam masala are the maestros, conducting a flavor orchestra that's both bold and harmonious.

Culinary Traditions, Passed Down Through Generations

Clay Pot Magic: Many Sindhi dishes are cooked in clay pots, which impart a unique earthy flavor.

A Fusion of Techniques: From deep-frying to slow-cooking, Sindhi chefs employ a diverse range of techniques.

A Symphony of Accompaniments: Chutneys, pickles, and raitas add a burst of flavor and texture to every meal.

A Feast for the Fingers: Many Sindhi dishes are traditionally eaten with the hands, a practice that fosters a sense of community and togetherness.

A Culinary Heritage, Cherished and Celebrated

Food is an integral part of Sindhi culture. Festivals like Diwali, Holi, and Eid are marked by special feasts and traditional dishes. Weddings and other family gatherings are occasions to celebrate with a sumptuous spread of food.

By sharing these culinary traditions, we can not only savor the flavors of Sindhi cuisine but also appreciate the rich cultural heritage that it represents.

A Confluence of Tastes: Cultural Influences and Culinary Fusion in Sindhi Cuisine

Sindh, a region steeped in history and vibrant culture, boasts a culinary tradition as rich and diverse as its heritage. Imagine a land where the aromas of fragrant spices mingle with the salty tang of the sea, where flavors dance on your tongue, a testament to centuries of cultural exchange. This is the essence of Sindhi cuisine, a unique tapestry woven from the threads of Arabic, Persian, and Indian influences.

A Culinary Crossroads

The story of Sindhi food is a tale of confluence, a culinary crossroads where civilizations met and mingled, leaving their indelible mark on the region's gastronomy.

The Arabic Influence: In the 7th century, Arab traders and conquerors arrived, bringing with them the treasures of the Middle East. Saffron, the "golden spice," began to imbue dishes with its distinctive aroma and color. Cumin, coriander, and cardamom added warmth and complexity. Biryani, a dish fit for royalty, made its grand entrance, along with the fragrant pilaf and succulent kebabs.

The Persian Touch: Around the same time, the Persian Empire extended its reach to Sindh, introducing a new wave of culinary artistry. Apricots, pomegranates, and almonds brought a touch of sweetness and elegance. Grilling and roasting techniques added a smoky depth to meats and vegetables. The Persians, like the Arabs, were enamored with saffron, cumin, coriander, and cardamom, further solidifying their place in Sindhi cuisine.

The Indian Connection: Sindh's proximity to India created a natural flow of culinary exchange. Hearty dals, fluffy rotis, and pillowy naans became staples. The fiery heat of chili peppers, the earthy warmth of turmeric, and the invigorating zest of ginger added new dimensions of flavor. Saag, palak paneer, and chana masala, beloved Indian dishes, found a welcome home in Sindhi kitchens.

A Journey Through Time

The Silk Road, that ancient artery of trade and cultural exchange, played a pivotal role in shaping Sindhi cuisine. Imagine caravans laden with exotic spices, traversing vast distances, bringing the flavors of the East and West to Sindh. This culinary melting pot simmered and evolved over centuries, influenced by the ebb and flow of empires and kingdoms.

A Symphony of Flavors

Sindhi cuisine is a symphony of flavors, a harmonious blend of spices and ingredients that tantalize the taste buds. The cuisine is generous and satisfying, with a focus on meat, seafood, and vegetables.

Signature Dishes: Sindhi biryani, a fragrant rice dish laden with meat, vegetables, and spices, is a true celebration of flavor. Sindhi pulao, cooked in ghee with aromatic spices, is comfort food at its finest. Sindhi karahi, a sizzling meat or vegetable dish in a spicy tomato sauce, is a testament to the region's love for bold flavors. And who can resist the succulent Sindhi kebabs, grilled to perfection?

Keeping the Tradition Alive

To experience the true essence of Sindhi cuisine is to embark on a culinary adventure. Here are ways to celebrate and preserve this rich heritage:

Culinary Workshops: Immerse yourself in the art of Sindhi cooking, learning the secrets of spice blending and traditional techniques.
Food Festivals: Gather with fellow food enthusiasts to savor the diverse flavors of Sindh, from savory curries to delectable sweets.

Sindhi cuisine is a treasure trove of flavors, a testament to the region's rich history and cultural diversity. Let us savor its unique blend of spices, celebrate its culinary heritage, and keep this vibrant tradition alive for generations to come.

A Journey Through the Flavors of Sindh: A Culinary Adventure

Sindh, a land steeped in history and culture, offers a vibrant tapestry of culinary delights. Its cuisine is a delightful blend of flavors, influenced by its geography, history, and diverse communities. Let's embark on a flavorful journey through the regions of Sindh, exploring its unique culinary offerings.

Upper Sindh: Where Wheat and Lentils Reign Supreme

In the heart of Upper Sindh, where the landscape is painted with golden fields of wheat and lentils, the cuisine reflects the bounty of the land. Here, you'll find comforting dishes like meetho chawal, a sweet rice dish that tantalizes the taste buds, and sai bhaji, a spinach curry that's both nutritious and delicious. And who can resist the crispy

delight of dal pakwan, a lentil soup served with crispy flatbread?
Image of Meetho Chawal, a sweet rice dish from Upper SindhOpens

Meetho Chawal, a sweet rice dish from Upper Sindh

Central Sindh: A Meat Lover's Paradise

As you venture into Central Sindh, the aroma of succulent meats fills the air. This region is renowned for its Sindhi biryani, a fragrant rice dish cooked with tender meat and a medley of spices. For a hearty meal, indulge in paya, a flavorful lamb trotter stew that will leave you wanting more. And don't forget to savor the classic khichri, a comforting dish of rice and lentils cooked to perfection.
Image of Sindhi Biryani, a rice dish cooked with meat and spicesOpens

Sindhi Biryani, a rice dish cooked with meat and spices

Lower Sindh: A Coastal Symphony of Flavors

The coastal region of Lower Sindh is a seafood lover's dream. Here, the cuisine is infused with the freshness of the Arabian Sea. Dive into a plate of Sindhi karahi, a spicy and tangy curry made with chicken or meat, or relish the catch of the day, prepared with local herbs and spices. And for those with a sweet tooth, the region offers delectable treats made with dates and jaggery, a local sweetener.

Beyond Regional Boundaries: A Tapestry of Cultures

Sindh's culinary landscape is further enriched by its diverse communities, each contributing its unique flavors to the mix. The Mohajir community, with roots in India, has introduced a variety of dishes from the subcontinent, while the Baloch community brings influences from Afghanistan and Iran.

A Culinary Map: Unveiling Sindh's Hidden Gems

To truly appreciate the culinary diversity of Sindh, imagine a culinary map that guides you through its regional specialties and hidden gems. This map would not only showcase the iconic dishes but also highlight the stories behind them, connecting you to the heart and soul of Sindh's culinary heritage.

Preserving and Promoting Sindh's Culinary Heritage

The traditional knowledge and culinary expertise of Sindh's communities are invaluable treasures. By documenting and preserving these traditions, we can ensure that future generations continue to savor the authentic flavors of Sindh. Culinary festivals, workshops, and online platforms can play a vital role in promoting Sindh's cuisine to a wider audience.

Embark on a Culinary Adventure

Sindh's culinary scene is an invitation to embark on a flavorful adventure. Whether you're exploring the wheat fields of Upper Sindh, savoring the meaty delights of Central Sindh, or indulging in the coastal flavors of Lower Sindh, each bite will tell a story of tradition, culture, and the passion for good food. So, come and discover the culinary treasures of Sindh, where every dish is a celebration of flavors.

A Culinary Caravan: The Journey of Sindhi Foodways

Imagine a cuisine that carries within its spices the whispers of ancient civilizations, the echoes of a homeland lost, and the resilience of a people scattered across the globe. This is the story of Sindhi food, a culinary tradition that has not just survived but thrived in the face of displacement and diaspora.

From the Indus to the World:

Sindhi cuisine, born in the fertile cradle of the Indus River Valley, is a vibrant tapestry woven with threads of history, culture, and adaptation. When the Partition of India in 1947 tore through the subcontinent, it also fractured the Sindhi community, forcing many to leave their ancestral home. Yet, like seeds carried by the wind, they carried their culinary heritage with them, planting it in new soil and watching it blossom in unexpected ways.

A Symphony of Flavors:

In India, the heartland of the Sindhi diaspora, their cuisine embraced the vibrant spices and diverse ingredients of their new surroundings. Imagine the tang of kokum, a souring agent borrowed from Maharashtrian cuisine, adding a new dimension to traditional Sindhi curries.

Across the seas, in the bustling metropolis of Hong Kong, Sindhi traders infused their dishes with Cantonese influences. Picture "Sai Bhaji," a humble spinach stew, transformed with the addition of Chinese greens and a whisper of oyster sauce.

In the United Kingdom, Sindhi cuisine found a new audience, adapting to British palates with milder curries and crispy "Aloo Tuk" that became a takeaway favorite.

And in North America, a new generation of Sindhi descendants is rediscovering their culinary roots, sparking a renaissance of traditional flavors and innovative interpretations.

Food as a Bridge to the Past:

For the Sindhi diaspora, food is more than sustenance; it's a powerful connection to their heritage, a living memory of their homeland. During festivals like Cheti Chand, the Sindhi New Year, tables overflow with traditional dishes, each bite a story, each aroma a reminder of their roots.

Family recipe books, passed down through generations, become treasured heirlooms, not just for the instructions they contain but for the handwritten notes and memories scribbled in the margins.

A Global Culinary Tapestry:

Today, Sindhi cuisine is stepping onto the world stage. In London, "Jhoolay Lal" tantalizes diners with refined interpretations of classic dishes, while in New York, "Sindhu" elevates Sindhi flavors to new heights of sophistication.

From bustling cafes in Dubai to trendy food trucks in Toronto, Sindhi food is finding its place in the global culinary landscape, captivating taste buds and hearts.

Capturing the Essence:

Imagine a documentary film that follows this culinary caravan, tracing the journey of Sindhi food from its ancient origins to its vibrant present. Through intimate interviews with families, chefs, and food enthusiasts, we'd witness the power of food to preserve cultural identity and bridge generations.

We'd see grandmothers sharing cherished recipes, their hands kneading dough with the practiced rhythm of tradition. We'd witness the sizzle of spices in a wok, the vibrant colors of a Sindhi feast, and the joyful faces gathered around a shared table.

This is a story waiting to be told, a celebration of resilience, adaptation, and the enduring power of food to connect us to our past, our present, and our shared human experience.

Women of Sindh: Navigating Tradition and Change

Whispers of the Indus: The Enduring Spirit of Sindhi Women

The Indus River, a lifeline snaking through parched lands, has witnessed the rise and fall of empires, the birth and death of civilizations. But one constant remains: the unwavering spirit of Sindhi women, their lives woven into the very fabric of this ancient land. Their stories, often whispered in the courtyards and sung in folk songs, are a testament to their resilience, their creativity, and their enduring impact on Sindhi society.

Echoes of Ancient Power

Imagine the sun beating down on Mohenjo-daro, a city teeming with life thousands of years ago. Here, amidst the intricate network of streets and grand structures, women were not mere shadows. They were potters molding clay with skillful hands, traders bartering precious goods, and priestesses invoking the divine. Legends speak of Devi Leilama, a visionary leader who, in an era when most civilizations were in their infancy, established thriving guilds, her wisdom shaping the very foundation of Sindhi commerce.

The Sufi's Song and the Warrior's Cry

Centuries later, as the melodies of Islam intertwined with ancient traditions, Sindhi women continued to carve their own paths. In the heart of Sehwan Sharif, the soul-stirring verses of Lal Shahbaz Qalandar, a Sufi mystic who defied gender norms, filled the air. Her poetry, a beacon of love and rebellion, resonated with the marginalized and challenged the rigid structures of her time.

But this era wasn't just about spiritual devotion. Picture the courageous Mai Bhagi, a warrior queen who, sword in hand, led her tribe against oppressive rulers in the 18th century. Her battle cry echoed across the battlefield, a testament to the fierce spirit that burned within Sindhi women.

Under the Colonial Gaze

The arrival of the British cast a long shadow over Sindh, bringing with it new laws and social constraints. Yet, even in the face of colonial oppression, Sindhi women refused to be silenced. Begum Kulsoom Khatoon, a fiery orator, rallied women to the cause of independence, her words igniting a passion for freedom. And in the salt plains of Tharparkar, Bai Amrita Devi stood defiant, leading a peaceful protest against unjust laws, her courage inspiring generations to come.

Weaving a New Future

Today, the daughters of Sindh walk diverse paths. They are doctors, engineers, entrepreneurs, and artists, their contributions shaping a modernizing society. Yet, the echoes of their ancestors remain, a constant reminder of their strength and resilience.

Keeping the Stories Alive

To truly understand Sindh, one must listen to the voices of its women. Let us bring their stories to life through vibrant murals depicting their achievements, interactive museums where visitors can step into their shoes, and animated films that capture their struggles and triumphs. Let us ensure that the legacy of these remarkable women continues to inspire generations to come.

The Sindhi woman. She walks through centuries of folklore and literature, her image shimmering and shifting like a mirage in the desert heat. Sometimes a queen, defiant and proud, sometimes a tragic lover, swept away by fate. Always, undeniably, present.

Shah Latif's Seven Queens stride across the landscape of Sindhi consciousness. 1 Marvi, unyielding in the face of a king's desire. 2 Momal, whose beauty ignites a kingdom. Sassi, forever searching for her beloved Punhoon. 3 These are not just stories, but potent symbols woven into the fabric of Sindhi identity. They whisper of feminine strength, resilience, and the enduring power of love.
1. Sindhi Folk Tales in English
2. Umar Marvi
3. Sassui Punnhun
But the tapestry is complex, interwoven with threads of sorrow and societal constraint. Sohni, defying her family for a forbidden love, drowns in the swirling Indus, clutching a clay pot as her only lifeline. Lilan Chanesar, a princess who dares to love a commoner, meets a tragic end. These tales, soaked in melancholy, reflect the harsh realities women have faced, their desires often clashing with rigid societal norms.

Yet, even in tragedy, there's defiance. Rani Hemu, the warrior queen, challenges the Mughal empire, a beacon of female leadership in a patriarchal world. These stories, passed down through generations, become anthems of resistance, reminding Sindhi women that they are capable of extraordinary courage and strength.

Imagine a vibrant anthology, a kaleidoscope of voices. Poems that sing of love and loss, short stories that delve into the inner lives of women, plays that challenge societal norms. This anthology wouldn't just be a collection of words, but a living testament to the enduring spirit of Sindhi women.

It would feature the voices of contemporary writers like Attiya Dawood, whose poignant poetry explores themes of identity and social justice, and Fahmida Riaz, whose bold verses challenge patriarchy and celebrate female empowerment. Alongside them, the voices of lesser-known writers, their stories waiting to be discovered, their perspectives adding to the rich tapestry of Sindhi women's experiences.

This anthology would be a celebration, a reclamation, a mirror reflecting the multifaceted reality of Sindhi women – their strength, their struggles, their hopes, and their dreams. It would be a powerful tool for social change, inspiring future generations to break free from restrictive norms and embrace their full potential.

The Sindhi woman, no longer just a character in a story, but the author of her own destiny.

The Resilient Bloom: Sindhi Women Navigating Tradition and Change

Imagine a vibrant tapestry woven with threads of resilience, ambition, and unwavering spirit. This is the story of Sindhi women today, a story of navigating ancient traditions while striving for a brighter future. In the heart of Pakistan, where the Indus River flows and history whispers through ancient ruins, Sindhi women are challenging norms, breaking barriers, and blossoming despite the thorns of societal constraints.

Shadows on the Path: Challenges Endured

The journey of Sindhi women is not without its shadows. Many, especially in rural areas, find themselves trapped in a cycle of limited access to education, healthcare, and economic opportunities.

Education: Poverty, cultural norms, and a lack of schools cast a long shadow on a girl's chance to learn. Even when they do attend school, they often face discrimination, leading to higher dropout rates and limited opportunities for higher education. Child marriage, a deeply ingrained practice, further cuts short their educational journey, trapping them in a cycle of limited choices.

Healthcare: The right to health remains a distant dream for many Sindhi women. Inadequate healthcare facilities, particularly in rural areas, coupled with gender bias in treatment, result in poor health outcomes, high maternal mortality rates, and a lack of awareness about basic health and hygiene.

Economic Empowerment: Cultural norms and societal expectations often confine Sindhi women to the domestic sphere. Limited education and workplace discrimination further hinder their economic participation. Even when employed, they grapple with a significant wage gap, perpetuating a cycle of economic vulnerability.

Blooming Against the Odds: Triumphs and Achievements

Despite these challenges, Sindhi women are not merely victims of circumstance. They are agents of change, writing their own narratives of resilience and success.

Education as a Weapon: Literacy rates are steadily rising, with more girls enrolling in schools and pursuing higher education. These women, armed with knowledge and degrees, are challenging the status quo and inspiring generations to come.

Entrepreneurial Spirit: A new wave of Sindhi women entrepreneurs is emerging, defying traditional roles and contributing to the economic growth of their communities. Their businesses, born of innovation and determination, are creating jobs, generating income, and shattering glass ceilings.

Voices of Change: Sindhi women are raising their voices, demanding their rights and advocating for social justice. Women's organizations and movements, led by passionate individuals, are fighting for gender equality, challenging discriminatory practices, and empowering women to take control of their lives.

Nurturing the Bloom: The Role of Women's Organizations

Women's organizations act as vital catalysts in this transformation, providing support, resources, and a platform for collective action. They empower women through education and training, advocate for their rights, and build networks of solidarity. These organizations are instrumental in pushing for policy changes that address the unique needs and challenges of Sindhi women.

Seeds of Change: The Path Forward

To truly empower Sindhi women, we need to sow the seeds of change through research, advocacy, and community engagement.

Data-driven Solutions: Collecting and analyzing data on the specific challenges faced by Sindhi women is crucial for informing policy decisions and targeted interventions.

Listening to Their Voices: Engaging with Sindhi women and their communities through participatory research methods will ensure that solutions are grounded in their lived realities and priorities.

Building Capacity: Empowering women and their organizations through training and capacity-building initiatives will equip them with the tools and skills needed to advocate for their rights and participate in decision-making processes.

Advocacy for Policy Change: Advocating for gender-responsive policies at all levels of government is essential for creating an enabling environment where Sindhi women can thrive.

Conclusion: A Tapestry of Hope

The story of Sindhi women is a tapestry woven with threads of resilience, determination, and hope. Despite facing significant challenges, they are breaking barriers, achieving remarkable milestones, and contributing to the social and economic fabric of their communities. By investing in their education, healthcare, and economic empowerment, and by amplifying their voices, we can help them realize their full potential and create a more just and equitable society for all.

Agents of Change: Empowering Sindhi Women for the Future

In the heart of Pakistan, nestled along the mighty Indus River, lies Sindh, a province rich in culture and tradition. Here, amidst the bustling cities and serene villages, reside the Sindhi women – resilient, resourceful, and ready to embrace the future. This isn't just a story of statistics and programs; it's about the dreams of Fatima, the determination of Ayesha, and the quiet strength of Rani, who, against all odds, are weaving a new narrative for themselves and their community.

Education as a Catalyst for Change: Where Knowledge Ignites Hope

Imagine a young girl, her eyes sparkling with curiosity, denied the chance to learn, her potential dimmed by societal constraints. This is the reality for many girls in Sindh, where access to education remains a formidable challenge. Yet, a wave of change is sweeping across the province, carried by initiatives that are breaking down barriers and opening doors to a brighter future.

The Sindh Education Foundation (SEF) is a beacon of hope, providing scholarships, building schools, and empowering teachers. Picture Fatima, a girl from a remote village, who, thanks to an SEF scholarship, is now the first in her family to attend school. Her journey is a testament to the transformative power of education.

Economic Empowerment: Breaking Barriers, Building Dreams

Economic independence is the key to unlocking a woman's true potential. In Sindh, women like Ayesha are challenging traditional norms and venturing into the world of entrepreneurship. With the support of microfinance programs like the Akhuwat Foundation, Ayesha has started her own small business, selling handcrafted jewelry. Her story is one of resilience, creativity, and the unwavering pursuit of financial freedom.

Political Participation: Amplifying Women's Voices
For too long, women's voices have been silenced in the
political arena. But in Sindh, women like Rani are stepping
up, demanding their rightful place at the decision-making
table. Organizations like the Women Democratic Front
(WDF) are providing a platform for women to engage in
the political process, advocating for their rights and
shaping policies that impact their lives.

The Digital Frontier: Navigating the Opportunities and
Challenges
The internet has revolutionized the world, connecting
people across borders and cultures. For Sindhi women, it's
a double-edged sword, offering opportunities for
education and connection, but also posing risks like
cyberbullying and online harassment. It's crucial to equip
women with the knowledge and tools to navigate this
digital landscape safely and responsibly.

Mentorship and Leadership: Nurturing the Leaders of
Tomorrow
Mentorship is a powerful tool for empowerment. Imagine
a young woman, unsure of her path, finding guidance
and support from a seasoned leader. Programs like LEAD,
run by the Aga Khan Foundation, are nurturing the next
generation of female leaders, providing them with the skills
and confidence to make a difference in their
communities.

Conclusion: A Tapestry of Hope and Resilience
The story of Sindhi women is one of resilience,
determination, and unwavering hope. They are breaking
barriers, challenging norms, and creating a brighter future
for themselves and generations to come. By investing in
their education, economic empowerment, and political
participation, we can help them unleash their full potential
and build a more equitable and prosperous society for all.

The Sufi Lyrical Tradition: Poetry as a Path to the Divine

Masters of Verse: Unveiling the Soul of Sindh through Sufi Poetry

The arid plains and vibrant culture of Sindh, a region nestled in the heart of modern-day Pakistan, have given birth to a rich tapestry of Sufi poetry. These mystical verses, imbued with spiritual longing and divine love, have profoundly shaped Sindh's cultural and intellectual landscape. Let's delve into the lives and legacies of three iconic Sufi poets who illuminated the path of divine love and social justice: Shah Abdul Latif Bhittai, Sachal Sarmast, and Qalandar Lal Shahbaz.

Shah Abdul Latif Bhittai (1689-1752): The Poet of the People

Imagine a world where poetry flows like the mighty Indus River, carrying the hopes, dreams, and sorrows of a people. This is the world of Shah Abdul Latif Bhittai, a Sufi mystic whose verses resonate with the soul of Sindh. His magnum opus, the "Risalo," is a collection of 328 soul-stirring verses that explore themes of love, devotion, social justice, and the human condition.

Bhittai's poetry, written in the mellifluous Latifi dialect, is a symphony of metaphors and similes, painting vivid pictures of the natural world and the inner landscape of the human heart. His verses are both profound and accessible, embracing the common man and the Sufi mystic with equal warmth. Bhittai's legacy transcends the boundaries of faith and language, making him a beloved figure in Sindh and beyond.

Sachal Sarmast (1739-1829): The Ecstatic Mystic

Sachal Sarmast, the "Truthful Ecstatic," was a poet of paradox, weaving together mystical insights, philosophical musings, and witty observations. His poetry, often sung in the captivating Kafi form, is a testament to his deep connection with the divine and his sharp critique of social injustice.

Sachal's verses are a whirlwind of emotions, ranging from ecstatic joy to profound sorrow. He fearlessly challenged the status quo, denouncing oppression and championing the cause of the marginalized. His poetry is a beacon of hope, reminding us that even in the darkest of times, the human spirit can soar to unimaginable heights.

Qalandar Lal Shahbaz (1660-1748): The Saint of Tolerance

Qalandar Lal Shahbaz, a disciple of Bhittai, carried the torch of Sufi poetry with his unique blend of mysticism, social commentary, and interfaith dialogue. His verses, infused with compassion and wisdom, called for unity and understanding in a world often divided by religious and social barriers.

Qalandar's poetry is a testament to his unwavering belief in the power of love to transcend all boundaries. He embraced people of all faiths, advocating for a society where everyone could live in harmony and peace. His legacy continues to inspire those who seek to build bridges of understanding and promote a more inclusive world.

Unique Voices in the Chorus of Sufi Poetry

Each of these poets brought their unique voice to the rich tradition of Sindhi Sufi poetry. Bhittai's lyrical beauty, Sachal's ecstatic fervor, and Qalandar's message of tolerance created a symphony of voices that continues to echo through the ages. Their poetry not only enriched the Sufi lyrical tradition but also provided a platform for social commentary and spiritual exploration.

Poetry as a Mirror of Society

The poetry of these Sufi masters emerged during a turbulent period in Sindh's history. The Mughal Empire's rule brought with it social unrest, political instability, and economic disparity. The Sufi poets, with their deep empathy for the common man, used their verses to express the pain and suffering of the people, while also offering messages of hope and resilience.

Their poetry also reflected the rich cultural and religious diversity of Sindh. Drawing inspiration from Islamic, Hindu, and other spiritual traditions, they created a tapestry of verses that celebrated the unity of all beings. Their message of tolerance and interfaith dialogue remains relevant even today, as we strive to build a more inclusive and harmonious world.

Preserving the Legacy: A Digital Tapestry of Sindhi Sufi Poetry

To ensure that the legacy of these Sufi poets continues to inspire future generations, we must embrace the power of technology. Imagine a digital archive where their verses come alive, translated into multiple languages, accompanied by soulful melodies, and enriched with critical analyses. This digital tapestry would not only preserve their poetry but also provide a platform for scholars, students, and poetry enthusiasts to engage with their timeless wisdom.

This archive could include interactive maps tracing the poets' journeys, audio recordings of renowned singers performing their verses, and even virtual reality experiences that transport users to the historical and cultural contexts in which the poetry was born. By embracing technology, we can weave a vibrant tapestry of Sindhi Sufi poetry that will continue to inspire and enlighten for generations to come.

Conclusion: The Enduring Legacy of Sindh's Sufi Poets

The Sufi poets of Sindh, with their profound spirituality, lyrical beauty, and social consciousness, have left an indelible mark on the world of literature. Their verses continue to resonate with people from all walks of life, offering solace, inspiration, and a glimpse into the depths of the human soul. By preserving and promoting their legacy, we can ensure that their timeless wisdom continues to illuminate the path towards a more just, compassionate, and harmonious world.

Subtopic 2: Love, Longing, and the Divine: A Journey Through the Soul of Sindhi Sufi Poetry

Introduction

Imagine a poetry tradition so rich and vibrant that it transcends the boundaries of language and culture, speaking directly to the soul. This is the magic of Sindhi Sufi poetry, a tradition that weaves together the threads of love, longing, and the divine into a tapestry of exquisite beauty.

This poetry isn't just about pretty words; it's a spiritual journey. It's about the yearning of the human heart for something beyond itself, for a connection with the divine that is often expressed through the metaphor of love. Think of the Sufi poet as a soul-traveler, using words to map the terrain of the heart and illuminate the path towards spiritual enlightenment.

A Love Story for the Ages

At the heart of Sindhi Sufi poetry lies the concept of love. But this isn't the kind of love you find in a romantic comedy. It's a love that burns with a fiery intensity, a love that consumes the lover and merges them with the Beloved, the divine.

One of the most powerful expressions of this love is the story of Laila and Majnun, a tale that has echoed through the centuries. Imagine two lovers, separated by the harsh realities of the world, yet united in a love that defies all boundaries. Their story is a mirror reflecting the soul's longing for union with the divine, a longing that transcends the physical realm.

The Longing of the Nightingale

But the journey towards divine love is not without its challenges. It's a path filled with longing, a yearning for something that seems just out of reach. This longing is beautifully captured in the poetry of Shah Abdul Latif, one of the greatest Sindhi Sufi poets.

Imagine the nightingale, pouring out its heart in song, yearning for the rose. This is the Sufi soul, longing for the divine, seeking union with the Beloved. It's a longing that is both painful and ecstatic, a bittersweet symphony that resonates with every heart that has ever yearned for something more.

The Divine: A Tapestry of Beauty

The divine in Sindhi Sufi poetry is not some distant, unapproachable entity. It's a living presence, a source of love, beauty, and compassion. It's the Beloved that the Sufi soul seeks, the ultimate goal of the spiritual journey.

Imagine a tapestry woven with threads of light, love, and wisdom. This is the divine as envisioned by Sindhi Sufi poets. It's a reality that transcends our limited human understanding, yet it's something that we can experience through the depths of our own hearts.

A Language of Symbols

To express these profound spiritual experiences, Sindhi Sufi poets use a language rich in metaphors and symbols. They draw inspiration from the natural world, from everyday life, and from the rich traditions of Islam.

Imagine the rose, a symbol of divine beauty and love. Or the nightingale, pouring out its heart in longing for the Beloved. These symbols, and many others, are the threads that weave together the tapestry of Sindhi Sufi poetry.

A Chorus of Voices

Sindhi Sufi poetry is not a monolithic tradition. It's a chorus of voices, each with its own unique perspective. Different Sufi orders and philosophical traditions have influenced the development of Sindhi Sufi poetry, adding to its richness and diversity.

Bringing Poetry to Life

But Sindhi Sufi poetry is not just meant to be read on a page. It's meant to be experienced, to be shared, to be brought to life. Imagine a poetry reading, where the verses of the Sufi poets are recited, their words resonating with the hearts of the listeners. Or a discussion group, where people come together to explore the depths of meaning within these poems.

These are just some of the ways that we can keep the tradition of Sindhi Sufi poetry alive, ensuring that its message of love, longing, and the divine continues to inspire and uplift souls for generations to come.

Conclusion

Sindhi Sufi poetry is more than just words on a page; it's a journey into the depths of the human soul. It's a testament to the power of love, the persistence of longing, and the enduring beauty of the divine. It's a tradition that has much to offer anyone seeking spiritual insight and inspiration, a beacon of light guiding us towards a deeper understanding of ourselves and the world around us.

So, let us immerse ourselves in the beauty of Sindhi Sufi poetry, and allow its words to awaken the divine spark within our own hearts.

Sindhi Sufi poetry, oh, it's more than just a spiritual voyage! It's a vibrant tapestry woven with threads of social and political commentary. Think of it as a secret language, whispering truths about injustice, oppression, and the masks of religious hypocrisy. These poets, like Shah Abdul Latif Bhittai and Sachal Sarmast, were like the sharpest of knives, cutting through the illusions of their time.

Imagine them, these poets, as fearless storytellers. They used metaphors, allegories, and parables like secret weapons. In "The Lament of the Weaver," Bhittai doesn't just tell you about a poor weaver struggling to survive; he paints a picture so vivid you can almost feel the weight of the loom on the weaver's tired shoulders. He makes you feel the sting of injustice, the way it traps people in poverty.

And then there's the hypocrisy, the kind that makes your blood boil. Bhittai, in "The Dervish and the Dog," shows us a holy man, chased away by a dog! It's a hilarious image, but it cuts deep. It exposes those who preach piety while their hearts are filled with darkness.

But these poets weren't just about criticism. Their words were like seeds of change. They championed education, hard work, and justice. They wanted a better world, and their poetry was their way of fighting for it.

Think of their poetry as a mirror reflecting the society of their time. They used their words to make people see the pain of others, to awaken their compassion. And they did it with such beauty and skill, their verses weaving magic that touched the soul.

Now, imagine bringing this poetry into the classroom. Imagine students, their eyes wide with wonder, debating the meaning of Bhittai's "Blind Man and the Elephant." They'd learn about different perspectives, about how truth can be elusive. They'd learn to think critically, to question, to challenge. And maybe, just maybe, they'd be inspired to become poets of change themselves.

Sindhi Sufi poetry is a treasure trove, a gift that keeps on giving. It's a source of wisdom, a call to action, and a testament to the power of art to change the world. It's a reminder that even in the darkest of times, the human spirit can soar, fueled by the fire of love, compassion, and the pursuit of justice.

A Tapestry of Soul: The Enduring Legacy of Sindhi Sufi Poetry

A Whispered Word, A World Transformed

Imagine a world where words aren't just ink on paper, but threads of cosmic consciousness. A world where poetry isn't a mere literary device, but a living, breathing entity, capable of stirring hearts and souls. This is the world of Sindhi Sufi poetry, a legacy that continues to captivate and inspire, weaving its magic through generations.

The Poets' Canvas: Painting Dreams in Verse

The likes of Shah Abdul Latif Bhittai and Sachal Sarmast weren't mere poets; they were mystics, philosophers, and revolutionaries, painting their dreams and aspirations onto the canvas of the human soul. Their verses, a blend of divine love, earthly longing, and cosmic consciousness, have echoed through the ages, transcending the boundaries of time and space.

A Symphony of Soul: The Music of Sufi Poetry

Sufi poetry isn't just meant to be read; it's meant to be felt. It's meant to be sung, to be danced, to be lived. The soulful melodies of Sufi kalam, with their intricate rhythms and heartfelt lyrics, have given birth to a rich musical tradition in Sindh. From the serene Kafi to the energetic Kalam, the music of Sufi poetry is a testament to the power of human expression.

A Tapestry Woven Through Time: The Enduring Influence

The influence of Sindhi Sufi poetry extends far beyond the realm of literature and music. It has shaped the very fabric of Sindhi culture, infusing it with a spirit of tolerance, compassion, and universal love. The shrines of Sufi saints have become pilgrimage sites, where people from all walks of life gather to seek solace, inspiration, and a deeper connection with the divine.

A Digital Renaissance: Preserving the Legacy

In our increasingly digital age, technology has emerged as a powerful tool for preserving and promoting the legacy of Sindhi Sufi poetry. Online platforms and digital libraries have made these timeless verses accessible to a global audience, transcending geographical boundaries. Social media has become a vibrant space for sharing, discussing, and celebrating Sufi poetry, fostering a sense of community among enthusiasts worldwide.

A Call to the Heart: Reclaiming the Sufi Spirit

In a world often characterized by division and conflict, the message of Sufi poetry offers a beacon of hope. It reminds us of our shared humanity, our interconnectedness, and the ultimate reality that lies beyond the veil of illusion. By embracing the teachings of Sufi saints, we can cultivate a more compassionate, just, and harmonious world.

Let's embark on a journey through the timeless verses of Sindhi Sufi poetry, and let their wisdom illuminate our souls.

Would you like to delve deeper into the life and works of a specific Sufi poet?

Perhaps you're curious about the impact of Sufi music on contemporary culture?

Or maybe you're interested in exploring the role of technology in preserving this rich heritage?

New Voices, New Visions: Modern Trends in Sindhi Literature

Subtopic 1: Breaking Boundaries: The Rise of New Literary Forms in Sindhi Literature

Imagine the Indus River, a lifeline for Sindh, its waters carrying not just silt and life, but stories whispered on the wind, sung by boatmen, and etched onto ancient palm leaves. For centuries, Sindhi literature flowed along a familiar course, nourished by the rich soil of Sufi poetry and folk tales. But the winds of change were stirring. The 20th century brought a tempest, a collision of tradition and modernity, giving rise to a flood of new literary forms that would forever alter the landscape of Sindhi letters.

The Seeds of Change

Mirza Kalichbeg, a scholar with a restless spirit, dared to dream of a new vessel for Sindhi stories. In 1876, he birthed Shah Jo Risalo, the first Sindhi novel. Imagine the whispers in the literary circles! A story not confined to verse, but sprawling across pages, weaving history and fiction into a tapestry of the life of Shah Abdul Latif. Kalichbeg, a pioneer, faced skepticism and scorn, yet he persevered, opening a door for generations to come.

The novel wasn't alone. Short stories, like nimble sparrows, began to flit across the literary scene. Ghulam Rabbani Agro, with his piercing gaze, captured the lives of ordinary people, their struggles with poverty and injustice etched in his stark prose. Jamal Abro, a master of psychological nuance, delved into the inner turmoil of characters grappling with identity and loss. These were stories that throbbed with the pulse of modern life, reflecting the anxieties and aspirations of a society in flux.

And then came the drama, bursting onto the stage with the energy of a Sindhi dhol. Aziz Kingrani, a playwright with a rebellious streak, used his pen as a weapon against social ills, his dialogues crackling with wit and defiance. Taj Mohammad Amrohi, a weaver of words, crafted intricate plays exploring the complexities of human relationships, love and betrayal playing out under the harsh glare of the spotlight.

Whispers from the West

The winds of change carried whispers from distant shores. Western literature, with its bold experiments and unflinching realism, seeped into the Sindhi consciousness. Charles Dickens, with his sprawling narratives and social critiques, found an echo in the works of writers like (insert a Sindhi writer who reflects Dickens' influence - research needed). Leo Tolstoy's exploration of the human spirit resonated with those seeking to delve into the depths of Sindhi identity. Even the haunting surrealism of Kafka found its way into the works of young writers grappling with the absurdity of the modern world.

Modernism, with its rejection of rigid forms and embrace of ambiguity, sparked a fire in the hearts of many Sindhi writers. They experimented with stream-of-consciousness, fragmented narratives, and free verse, pushing the boundaries of language and form. This wasn't mere imitation; it was a dialogue, a vibrant exchange between tradition and innovation.

Guardians of the Flame: Literary Journals and Publishing Houses

In the bustling city of Karachi and the quiet towns along the Indus, literary journals emerged as guardians of the flame, nurturing new talent and fanning the fires of creativity. Sindhi Adabi Sangat, with its venerable journal Sindh, became a platform for established and emerging voices. Kitab, its pages filled with experimental poetry and provocative essays, challenged readers to expand their horizons.

Sindhi Sangat championed a different vision, its journal Gulzar-e-Sindh celebrating the beauty and richness of Sindhi language and culture. Shehr, with its urban focus, captured the pulse of a rapidly changing society.

These journals weren't just platforms; they were battlegrounds where literary debates raged, where new ideas were forged, and where the future of Sindhi literature was shaped.

Festivals of the Word

Imagine the vibrant energy of the International Sindhi Literary Festival: a kaleidoscope of colors, languages, and ideas. Writers from across the globe gather to celebrate the written word, their voices mingling with the strains of traditional music. Young poets, their eyes shining with passion, recite their verses, their words echoing through the halls. Seasoned novelists engage in lively discussions, their insights sparking new perspectives.

The Sindh Youth Festival, a whirlwind of youthful energy, showcases the talent of the next generation. Short story competitions ignite friendly rivalries, while drama performances bring stories to life under the open sky.

These festivals are more than just events; they are crucibles where creativity is forged, where connections are made, and where the future of Sindhi literature is nurtured.

A River Still Flowing

The journey of Sindhi literature is a testament to the enduring human spirit, its capacity to adapt, innovate, and create. From the ancient bards to the modern novelists, the river of Sindhi literature continues to flow, its waters enriched by new voices, new forms, and new perspectives. As technology and globalization reshape our world, Sindhi writers will undoubtedly continue to explore new frontiers, their words carrying the echoes of the past while charting a course for the future.

This is just a glimpse into the vibrant world of Sindhi literature. To truly understand its depth and complexity, one must dive into its waters, explore its currents, and immerse oneself in its stories.

Let's breathe life into this exploration of Sindhi literature! Imagine stepping into a bustling Karachi marketplace, the air thick with the scent of spices and the sounds of vendors hawking their wares. Amidst the chaos, a young woman with kohl-rimmed eyes clutches a worn paperback, her face illuminated by the words of Kala Prakash. In Waqt Withuoon ain Wichotiyoon, Prakash doesn't just tell us about the struggles of modern Sindhi women; she throws us right into the heart of their lives. We feel the protagonist's frustration as she navigates the expectations of her traditional family while yearning for independence in the sprawling metropolis.

But Prakash isn't alone. Across the Indus River, in a quiet village nestled amidst mango groves, Lal Pushp pens stories that resonate with the raw realities of rural Sindh. In Bandhan ain Arman, his words are like a whispered cry against injustice, echoing the pain of a young bride forced into a marriage that shackles her spirit. Pushp, a former school teacher with a deep empathy for the marginalized, doesn't shy away from depicting the harsh truths of gender inequality and domestic violence.

And then there's Faiz Mohammad Faiz, the poet whose verses flow like the mighty Indus itself. In Sindh ji Maati, his lament for the ravaged environment is a call to action, a plea to protect the land that has nurtured generations of Sindhis. "The once fertile fields now thirst," he writes, his words painting a stark picture of a land parched by drought and choked by pollution.

These are just a few of the voices that make up the vibrant tapestry of contemporary Sindhi literature. They are storytellers, poets, and playwrights who hold up a mirror to society, reflecting its triumphs and its struggles. They give voice to the voiceless, challenge the status quo, and inspire hope for a better future.

But what if we could bring these voices together? Imagine a digital platform, a vibrant online space called "Sindh Speaks," where writers could share their work, connect with readers, and engage in lively discussions. This platform wouldn't just be a repository of texts; it would be a living, breathing community. Picture this:

Interactive maps showcasing the locations that inspire these stories, allowing users to virtually explore the landscapes of Sindh.

Audio recordings of poets reciting their verses in the rich cadence of the Sindhi language, bringing their words to life.

Live Q&A sessions with authors, where readers can delve deeper into the themes and motivations behind their work.

Translation projects making Sindhi literature accessible to a global audience, fostering cultural exchange and understanding.

"Sindh Speaks" would be more than just a website; it would be a portal into the heart and soul of Sindh, a testament to the power of literature to connect, inspire, and transform. It would be a space where the timeless traditions of Sindhi storytelling merge with the boundless possibilities of the digital age, ensuring that these voices continue to resonate for generations to come.

Imagine a bustling street market in Karachi, the air thick with the aroma of spices and the sounds of hawkers calling out their wares. Amidst the chaos, a young boy, no older than ten, clutches a worn paperback close to his chest. He's captivated by the tales of brave warriors and mystical creatures, his imagination ignited by the words of Shah Abdul Latif Bhittai, the Sufi poet whose verses have echoed through Sindh for centuries. This boy, like generations before him, is being transported to another world through the magic of Sindhi literature.

But this is not just a story of the past. In a quiet café in London, a young woman sips her chai latte while scrolling through Instagram. A post catches her eye – a striking image of a woman in traditional Sindhi dress, accompanied by a poem in both Sindhi and English. It's the work of a diaspora writer, her words bridging continents and cultures. With a click, the woman in the café is connected to a community of Sindhi writers and readers across the globe, a testament to how globalization has woven new threads into the tapestry of this ancient literary tradition.

Globalization, a force that has reshaped our world, has also breathed new life into Sindhi literature. It's a story of both opportunity and challenge, of preserving a unique identity while embracing the interconnectedness of our modern age.

Whispers of the Past, Echoes of the Future

Sindhi literature, woven from the threads of Sufi mysticism, folklore, and the rich history of the Indus Valley civilization, carries within it the soul of a people. Think of the vibrant colors of a Sindhi ajrak, each intricate pattern telling a tale of resilience, creativity, and a deep connection to the land.

But as Sindhis migrated across the globe, carrying their stories and traditions with them, their literature began to reflect the complexities of diaspora. Writers like Sundri Uttamchandani, based in Spain, explore the poignant experience of straddling two worlds – the nostalgia for a homeland left behind and the challenges of forging a new identity in a foreign land. Her words are a poignant reminder of the emotional landscape of migration, the constant push and pull between belonging and displacement.

"My heart beats with the rhythm of the Sindhu River," writes Uttamchandani, "even though I stand on the shores of the Mediterranean."

A Global Stage for Sindhi Voices

Globalization has not only dispersed Sindhi voices but has also amplified them. Through translations, literary festivals, and the power of the internet, Sindhi literature is finding new audiences and engaging in exciting cross-cultural dialogues.

Imagine the Karachi Literature Festival, a vibrant hub where Sindhi writers share the stage with authors from around the world. Ideas spark, stories intertwine, and the boundaries between cultures blur. This is globalization at its best – a celebration of diversity and a testament to the power of literature to connect us all.

Technology, too, has played a transformative role. Online platforms like "Kitab" and "Sindh Salamat" have become virtual meeting places for Sindhi writers and readers, transcending geographical barriers and fostering a sense of community. Social media has given writers a direct connection to their audience, allowing them to share their work, engage in discussions, and build a global following.

Preserving the Flame in a Digital Age

Yet, within this exciting evolution, there lies a challenge. How do Sindhi writers navigate the global landscape while preserving the essence of their literary heritage? How do they ensure that the Sindhi language, with its unique cadence and rich vocabulary, doesn't get lost in the sea of globalized communication?

These are questions that require thoughtful consideration and proactive solutions. We need to invest in language education, support the translation of Sindhi works, and encourage young people to engage with their literary roots.

A Call to Action

The future of Sindhi literature lies in our hands. Let us become its champions, sharing its beauty and wisdom with the world.

   Seek out Sindhi writers: Explore the works of both established and emerging authors.
   Support translations: Encourage the publication of Sindhi literature in multiple languages.

Embrace technology: Utilize online platforms to connect with Sindhi writers and readers worldwide.

Pass on the legacy: Share the love of Sindhi literature with future generations.

By nurturing this precious cultural heritage, we ensure that the stories, poems, and songs of Sindh continue to resonate for generations to come. Let the words of Shah Abdul Latif Bhittai, carried on the winds of globalization, inspire and enlighten the world.

Nurturing Creativity: Breathing Life into Sindhi Literature

Imagine a vibrant tapestry woven with threads of history, culture, and heartfelt expression. This tapestry is Sindhi literature, a treasure trove of stories, poems, and songs passed down through generations. Yet, this precious art form faces challenges in the modern world, struggling to be seen and heard amidst the clamor of mainstream voices.

The Struggles of the Sindhi Wordsmith

Sindhi writers, the weavers of this intricate tapestry, face hurdles that threaten their ability to create and share their work:

The Publisher's Dilemma: Imagine a passionate writer with a heart full of stories, but nowhere to share them. Many publishers prioritize commercially viable projects, leaving Sindhi writers with limited opportunities to bring their works to life.

The Weight of the World: Writing, especially in a less recognized language, often doesn't pay the bills. Sindhi writers often juggle multiple jobs, leaving little time and energy for their creative passions.

Hidden in Plain Sight: Despite its rich history, Sindhi literature often remains hidden from the national and international spotlight. This lack of recognition limits opportunities for Sindhi writers to reach wider audiences and gain the appreciation they deserve.

The Digital Divide: In today's digital age, not everyone has equal access to technology and online platforms. This can hinder Sindhi writers from participating in the evolving world of online literature and connecting with a global audience.

A Fading Voice: In some regions, the Sindhi language itself is fading, especially among younger generations. This poses a grave threat to the future of Sindhi literature.

Champions of Sindhi Literature

But there's hope! Various organizations and individuals are stepping up to support Sindhi writers and ensure the survival of this beautiful literary tradition:

Literary Guardians: Organizations like the Sindhi Language Authority and the Sindh Culture Department act as guardians of Sindhi literature, publishing books, organizing festivals, and providing much-needed support to writers.

Community Builders: NGOs and literary festivals, like the Sindh Literature Festival, bring together writers, poets, and readers, creating a vibrant community where Sindhi literature can flourish.
Government Support: The Sindh government provides financial aid, awards, and language promotion policies to encourage and recognize Sindhi writers.

Private Patrons: Corporations and individuals are also lending a helping hand, sponsoring events, funding publications, and providing scholarships to aspiring writers.

Embracing the Digital Age

The internet offers exciting new possibilities for Sindhi literature:

Social Media: Writers can connect with readers, share their work, and build a following on platforms like Facebook, Twitter, and Instagram.

Online Homes for Sindhi Literature: Blogs, websites, and online literary magazines provide spaces to showcase Sindhi writing to a global audience.
E-books and Self-Publishing: The rise of e-books empowers Sindhi writers to publish their work independently and reach readers directly.
Crowdfunding: Platforms like Kickstarter enable writers to raise funds for their projects and build a community of supporters.

A Call to Action: Creating a Literary Lifeline

To further support Sindhi writers, we need to create a dedicated literary fund or grant program. This fund would provide financial assistance for publishing, research, travel, and translation, ensuring that Sindhi literature continues to thrive.

Imagine a world where:

Sindhi writers have the resources they need to create and share their stories.
Sindhi literature is celebrated and recognized on a global stage.

Young generations embrace their literary heritage and carry it forward.

By working together, we can ensure that the tapestry of Sindhi literature continues to weave its magic for generations to come.

Sindhi in the Digital Age: Challenges and Opportunities for Language Survival

The digital revolution has undeniably reshaped the landscape of human communication, and the Sindhi language, much like others around the world, finds itself navigating this uncharted territory. Technology has brought about a profound transformation in how we interact, and the Sindhi language is no exception. Let's delve into the intricate ways in which technology is molding the Sindhi language, exploring the changes, challenges, and potential solutions for its preservation and promotion in the digital age.

Technology's Influence on Sindhi Language Use

Technology has brought about significant changes in the way Sindhi is used, impacting vocabulary, grammar, and communication styles.

Vocabulary: The digital world, with its influx of English and Urdu terms through social media and online platforms, has led to the adoption of many loanwords in Sindhi. While some view this as an enriching phenomenon, others express concern about the potential erosion of the language's unique identity. Words like "friend" (replacing "dost"), "online" (replacing "aan laain"), and "post" (replacing "mokool") have become commonplace in digital Sindhi communication. Additionally, new words have emerged to describe technology-related concepts, such as "computer" (ﮐﻤﭙﻴﻮﭨﺮ), "internet" (ﺍﻧﭩﺮﻧﻴﭧ), and "smartphone" (ﺳﻤﺎﺭﭦ ﻓﻮﻥ).

Grammar: The informal nature of digital communication has led to a relaxation of grammatical rules in Sindhi. Shortened forms, omissions of diacritical marks, and simplified sentence structures are common. For example, the possessive marker "jo" (جو) is often omitted in online chats, and the formal pronoun "tavaan" (توهان) is frequently replaced with the informal "toon" (تون). While this may enhance efficiency in fast-paced digital conversations, it also raises concerns about the potential degradation of grammatical accuracy in formal settings.

Communication Styles: The rise of emojis, GIFs, and memes has added new dimensions to Sindhi digital communication. These visual elements often convey emotions and sentiments more effectively than words, contributing to a more nuanced and expressive communication style. However, over-reliance on these visual cues can sometimes lead to misinterpretations and hinder the development of written communication skills.

Impact of Social Media and Online Platforms

Social media, messaging apps, and online platforms have accelerated the evolution of the Sindhi language and influenced dialectal variations.

Language Evolution: The rapid exchange of information and ideas on social media platforms like Facebook, Twitter, and Instagram has exposed Sindhi speakers to various linguistic influences, leading to the adoption of new words, phrases, and expressions. This constant interaction and exposure to different dialects and languages contribute to the dynamic evolution of the Sindhi language.

Dialectal Variation: While online platforms can bridge geographical barriers and connect Sindhi speakers from different regions, they can also accentuate dialectal differences. Online forums and groups often form based on regional affiliations, reinforcing distinct linguistic features and potentially leading to further divergence in dialects. For instance, the use of specific vocabulary and pronunciation differences between speakers from Hyderabad, Karachi, and Sukkur can become more pronounced in online interactions.

Challenges in Maintaining Linguistic Standards

The informal and dynamic nature of digital communication poses challenges to maintaining linguistic standards and orthographic consistency in Sindhi.

Lack of Standardization: The absence of a universally accepted Sindhi keyboard layout and the inconsistent use of diacritical marks contribute to orthographic variations. Different platforms and devices may offer different keyboard layouts, leading to inconsistencies in spelling and pronunciation.

Informal Language Use: The prevalence of informal language, abbreviations, and slang in digital communication can make it difficult to maintain formal linguistic standards. The use of "SMS language" with shortened forms and phonetic spellings can create confusion and hinder comprehension, especially for those unfamiliar with these informal conventions.

Limited Digital Resources: The availability of Sindhi language resources, such as dictionaries, grammar guides, and spell-checkers, is still limited in the digital realm. This scarcity of resources makes it challenging for users to verify spellings, learn proper grammar, and adhere to linguistic standards.

Practical Steps for Promoting Proper Sindhi Language Use

To address the challenges and promote proper Sindhi language use in digital communication, the following practical steps can be taken:

Standardized Keyboard Layout: Develop and promote a universally accepted Sindhi keyboard layout for all digital platforms and devices. This will ensure consistency in spelling and reduce orthographic variations.

Digital Language Resources: Create and disseminate comprehensive digital resources, including online dictionaries, grammar guides, and spell-checkers, to assist users in adhering to linguistic standards.

Language Awareness Campaigns: Launch public awareness campaigns to promote the importance of proper Sindhi language use in digital communication. Encourage the use of correct grammar, spelling, and punctuation, even in informal settings.

Educational Initiatives: Integrate digital Sindhi language learning in schools and universities to equip students with the necessary skills for effective online communication.

Community Engagement: Foster collaboration between linguists, educators, and technology developers to create engaging and informative online content that promotes proper Sindhi language use.

By implementing these measures, we can ensure that the Sindhi language thrives in the digital age, preserving its rich heritage while adapting to the evolving communication landscape.

Sindhi Language Learning in the Digital Age: A Vibrant Tapestry of Tools

The digital world is a bustling bazaar for language learners, overflowing with colorful tools and resources. And for those drawn to the melodic sounds of Sindhi, the options are plentiful and exciting! Let's dive into this digital treasure trove and explore how it can empower you on your Sindhi language journey.

1. Online Dictionaries: Your Pocket-Sized Language Guru

Imagine having a wise old scholar who whispers the meaning of any Sindhi word into your ear. That's what online dictionaries like Sindhi Online Dictionary and Rekhta Dictionary offer! They're your instant guides to a universe of words, complete with pronunciation tips and examples that bring the language to life.

But, like any wise guru, they have their quirks. Sometimes they might be a bit vague on the finer points of grammar, or miss the subtle cultural nuances that give words their true flavor.

2. Language Learning Apps: Your Playful Companions

Learning Sindhi doesn't have to be all serious study. Apps like Duolingo turn vocabulary drills into a game, with points and rewards that keep you coming back for more. Memrise uses clever memory tricks to help new words stick in your mind, while Babbel acts like a personal tutor, guiding you through structured lessons and giving you personalized feedback.

Think of them as friendly companions on your journey, each with their own personality and teaching style. They're great for picking up the basics, but remember, they can't replace the joy of real-life conversations and cultural immersion.

3. Interactive Platforms: Stepping into a Sindhi World

Ready to immerse yourself in the vibrant culture of Sindh? Interactive platforms like Sindhi Academy and Sindhi Online Learning are your portals to a virtual Sindhi world. They offer a rich tapestry of interactive lessons, quizzes, games, and forums where you can connect with fellow learners and native speakers.

Imagine exploring the bustling streets of Karachi, listening to traditional Sindhi music, or even participating in a virtual Sindhi wedding! These platforms offer a taste of authentic Sindhi life, making your language learning journey all the more enriching.

4. Choosing the Right Tools for Your Journey

With so many options, how do you choose the right tools for your Sindhi adventure? Consider these guiding stars:

    Content: Is it accurate, engaging, and culturally relevant?
    Features: Does it offer interactive exercises, games, and opportunities to connect with others?
    Accessibility: Is it suitable for your level and learning style?
    Cost: Is it affordable and good value for money?
    User Experience: Is it easy to use and navigate?

Remember, the best tools are the ones that inspire you to learn and make the journey enjoyable.

5. The Magic of VR and AR: A Glimpse into the Future

Imagine stepping into a virtual reality where you can wander through the ancient ruins of Mohenjo-daro, practice your Sindhi with virtual characters, or even attend a Sindhi festival! Virtual Reality (VR) and Augmented Reality (AR) are still emerging, but they hold the promise of truly immersive language learning experiences.

Think of them as magic carpets that transport you to another world, where you can learn Sindhi in a way that's both fun and unforgettable.

6. Preserving the Past, Embracing the Future

Digital archives and online libraries are like treasure chests, safeguarding the rich heritage of Sindhi literature and culture. Platforms like the Sindhi Academy Digital Library and the Sindhi Heritage Foundation Library offer a vast collection of books, manuscripts, poems, songs, and films, ensuring that the soul of Sindh is preserved for generations to come.

These digital repositories are not just about the past; they're also about building the future. They provide a space for Sindhi writers, artists, and scholars to share their work with the world, ensuring that the language continues to thrive in the digital age.

Embark on Your Sindhi Adventure!

The digital world offers a wealth of opportunities for anyone who wants to learn Sindhi. Whether you're a beginner or an advanced learner, there are tools and resources to help you achieve your goals. So, embrace the power of technology, immerse yourself in the beauty of Sindhi, and let your language learning journey be an exciting and fulfilling adventure!

Social Media: A Lifeline for Sindhi in the Digital Age

Imagine a bustling bazaar, filled with vibrant colors, the scent of spices, and the lively chatter of Sindhi. Now picture that bazaar fading away, the voices growing quieter, the stalls emptying. This is the very real threat facing the Sindhi language today. But amidst the encroaching silence, a new space is emerging where Sindhi can thrive – the digital world.

Social media platforms like Facebook, Twitter, and Instagram aren't just places for selfies and cat videos. They're becoming virtual bazaars, where Sindhi speakers gather to connect, share their culture, and breathe new life into their language.

Sindhi's Digital Champions

Think of the Sindhi Language Movement as a passionate group of storytellers huddled around a digital campfire, sharing folktales and proverbs in Sindhi, keeping those ancient embers glowing. The Sindhi Language Academy is like a vibrant online school, offering courses and resources to anyone wanting to learn the language. And the Sindhi Heritage Foundation? Imagine a virtual museum, brimming with historical photos, traditional music, and the works of Sindhi artists and writers.

These are just a few examples of how social media is becoming a lifeline for Sindhi, allowing it to flow beyond geographical boundaries and connect a global community.

Navigating the Digital Maze

But this digital landscape also presents challenges. English, like a powerful tide, threatens to overwhelm smaller languages. Code-switching, while a natural part of bilingualism, can sometimes lead to Sindhi being sidelined in online conversations.

How can we ensure Sindhi doesn't get lost in the digital noise? By making it irresistibly cool. Imagine Sindhi memes that go viral, witty Sindhi hashtags trending on Twitter, and Sindhi YouTubers captivating audiences with their creativity. It's about packaging the beauty and richness of Sindhi in a way that resonates with young people, making them proud to use it online.

Raising a Digital Battle Cry

Social media isn't just about sharing; it's about activism. The hashtag #EndangeredLanguages is a rallying cry, uniting language advocates worldwide. Imagine #SindhiLanguage trending globally, with people sharing Sindhi poetry, music, and art, raising awareness of its beauty and the threats it faces.

Social media can be a powerful megaphone, amplifying the voices of Sindhi speakers and inspiring a new generation of language warriors.

A Digital Toolkit for Sindhi

So, how can we harness the power of social media to ensure Sindhi thrives in the digital age? Here are a few ideas:

Hashtag Power: Imagine hashtags like #SindhiStories, #SindhiMusicMonday, or #LearnSindhi sparking online conversations and connecting people.

Content is King: Think captivating videos showcasing Sindhi culture, interactive quizzes testing language skills, and online storytelling sessions bringing Sindhi folktales to life.

Influencer Magic: Partnering with Sindhi musicians, artists, or YouTubers to promote the language to their followers.

Virtual Gatherings: Hosting online poetry slams, music festivals, or cooking demonstrations, creating a sense of community and shared passion for Sindhi.

It's about being creative, engaging, and giving young people a platform to express themselves in Sindhi.

In conclusion, social media is a powerful tool in the fight to revitalize Sindhi. It's a space where the language can evolve, connect with new audiences, and resist the forces that threaten its existence. Let's use it wisely, creatively, and passionately to ensure that the vibrant sounds of Sindhi continue to echo in the digital age and beyond.

Bridging the Digital Divide: Empowering Sindhi Voices in the Digital Age

Imagine a young Sindhi girl in a remote village, her eyes sparkling with curiosity. She dreams of becoming a doctor, but her village school lacks even basic science books, let alone the internet. This is the reality for many Sindhi speakers, where the digital divide isn't just a gap – it's a chasm that separates them from a world of opportunities.

The Digital Divide: A Silent Barrier to Progress

For Sindhi speakers, especially those in marginalized communities, the lack of technology access is like being trapped in a silent film while the world moves on to vibrant

Technicolor. This digital exclusion impacts their lives in profound ways:

Education becomes a distant dream: Without access to online resources, textbooks, or educational platforms, Sindhi students struggle to keep pace with their connected peers. Their thirst for knowledge is often quenched only by the limited resources available in their immediate surroundings.

Jobs of the future remain out of reach: In today's digital economy, where even basic tasks require internet access, Sindhi speakers find themselves at a disadvantage. They may lack the digital literacy needed to compete for jobs, further perpetuating cycles of poverty.

Social isolation deepens: While social media connects billions, many Sindhi speakers remain isolated, their voices unheard in the global conversation. This isolation can lead to feelings of disenfranchisement and exclusion.

Economic opportunities slip away: From farmers who could benefit from online agricultural information to artisans who could sell their crafts on e-commerce platforms, the lack of technology access hinders economic growth and self-sufficiency.

Building Bridges: A Collaborative Approach

The good news is that change is possible. By working together, governments, non-profits, and community organizations can weave a digital safety net for Sindhi speakers:

Government initiatives: Imagine the government launching programs that provide subsidized tablets pre-loaded with educational content in Sindhi. Picture community technology centers humming with activity as people learn essential digital skills. These are the kinds of initiatives that can make a real difference.

Non-profit organizations: Organizations can step in to provide not just technology but also culturally relevant digital literacy training. Imagine workshops where Sindhi-speaking women learn to use the internet to access healthcare information or start their own online businesses.

Community-based programs: Local libraries can be transformed into vibrant digital hubs, offering free internet access, computer classes, and even coding workshops for young people. Imagine a network of community volunteers who help seniors get online and connect with their families.

The Power of Mobile: A Gateway to the Digital World

Mobile phones are becoming increasingly ubiquitous, even in remote areas. This presents a golden opportunity to bridge the digital divide. Affordable data plans, coupled with user-friendly apps in Sindhi, can empower communities with access to information, education, and economic opportunities.

Practical Steps: Turning Vision into Reality

Partner with tech companies: Imagine technology providers donating refurbished laptops or offering discounted internet services to underserved communities.

Develop culturally relevant content: Imagine online educational resources in Sindhi, from interactive language learning apps to digital libraries filled with Sindhi literature.

Empower local champions: Identify and train tech-savvy individuals within Sindhi communities to become digital ambassadors, providing peer-to-peer support and training.

Conclusion: A Future Where Every Voice is Heard

Bridging the digital divide for Sindhi speakers is not just about providing technology; it's about empowering a community, amplifying their voices, and ensuring that they are not left behind in the digital age. It's about creating a future where a young Sindhi girl in a remote village can access the same opportunities as anyone else, and where her dreams, like her internet connection, know no bounds.

Globalization and its Discontents: Sindhi Culture at the Crossroads

Imagine Sindhi culture as a vibrant tapestry, woven with threads of ancient traditions, shimmering with the gold of its history. Now, imagine winds of globalization sweeping across this tapestry, bringing with them new colors and patterns. Some threads intertwine beautifully, creating unexpected and exciting designs, while others threaten to unravel the intricate patterns passed down through generations.

This is the reality of Sindhi culture today, a vibrant culture at a crossroads, navigating the dynamic interplay between global flows and local traditions.

The Global Bazaar:

Globalization has brought the world to Sindh's doorstep. English words pepper everyday conversations, Bollywood tunes mingle with traditional folk songs, and Western fashion trends find their way into local bazaars. It's like a bustling global bazaar where Sindhi youth, armed with smartphones, connect with the world, sharing their own culture and absorbing influences from across the globe. This exchange has birthed exciting new fusions - imagine the energy of Sindhi hip-hop, a vibrant blend of tradition and modernity, or the tantalizing flavors of Sindhi fusion cuisine, where local spices dance with global ingredients.

The Whispers of Ancestors:

Yet, amidst this exciting exchange, there's a quiet tension. The whispers of ancestors, carried through centuries-old traditions, seem to fade in the face of the global roar. Elders worry about the erosion of the Sindhi language, the soul of their culture. Will their grandchildren still sing the ancient folk songs, wear the traditional Ajrak, or understand the stories woven into their rich heritage?

This is the heart of the challenge - how to embrace the opportunities of globalization without losing the essence of Sindhi identity.

Weaving a New Narrative:

But the Sindhi spirit is resilient, like a date palm standing tall in the desert winds. The very forces that threaten to unravel the tapestry are also being used to strengthen it. Social media, once a symbol of global culture, has become a platform to showcase Sindhi poetry, music, and art. Museums and cultural centers, like treasure chests, are being revitalized to preserve and celebrate Sindhi heritage.

And in the heart of Sindh, festivals like the Sindh Festival burst with life. Imagine a sea of people, adorned in colorful traditional attire, celebrating their shared heritage. The air vibrates with the rhythm of the dhol, the mesmerizing twirls of Sufi dancers, and the aroma of traditional delicacies. It's a powerful reminder of the enduring spirit of Sindh, a culture that refuses to be lost in the global melting pot.

A Bridge Between Worlds:

Sindh is not just preserving its own culture, but also building bridges with the world. Cultural exchange programs, like threads of connection, weave together diverse cultures. Imagine students from around the world learning the Sindhi language, sharing their own cultural stories, and forging bonds of friendship that transcend borders.

This is the future Sindh is striving for - a future where globalization is not a threat, but an opportunity to share the beauty and richness of Sindhi culture with the world, while cherishing and preserving its unique identity. It's a story of resilience, adaptation, and the enduring power of culture to connect us all.

Sindh's Globalization Dance: A Tapestry of Opportunities and Challenges

Imagine Sindh as a vibrant dancer, twirling onto the world stage of globalization. This dance is full of energy and promise, but also requires careful balance and adaptation. Let's explore the intricate steps of this dance:

Opportunities: The Upbeat Rhythm

New Markets Beckon: Sindh's traditional goods, like exquisite textiles, fragrant rice, and finely crafted leather products, are no longer confined to local bazaars. They've waltzed their way into global markets, bringing back increased wealth and recognition. The China-Pakistan Economic Corridor (CPEC) acts as a grand bridge, connecting Sindh to even more customers and possibilities.

Investment Flows In: Foreign investors, intrigued by Sindh's potential, are pouring in capital, particularly into energy, infrastructure, and manufacturing. This investment is like a powerful drumbeat, driving job creation, technological leaps, and overall economic progress.

Technology's Guiding Hand: Globalization has gifted Sindh with access to cutting-edge technology and knowledge. This empowers local businesses to become more efficient, innovative, and competitive. It's like learning new, exciting dance moves to stay ahead in the global performance.

Remittances: A Lifeline from Abroad: As some Sindhis seek opportunities abroad, they send back remittances, a steady stream of financial support for their families and communities. This is like a safety net, ensuring economic stability while loved ones explore the world.

Challenges: The Unexpected Twists

Competition Heats Up: Globalization has thrown Sindh's businesses into a lively competition with international players. Small and medium-sized enterprises (SMEs), in particular, find themselves needing to perfect their steps to keep pace with larger, more experienced dancers.

Environmental Concerns Loom: The rapid industrialization and urbanization accompanying globalization have cast a shadow on Sindh's environment. Pollution, deforestation, and water scarcity are urgent issues that need addressing, ensuring the dance floor remains sustainable for future generations.

Income Inequality Widens: While globalization has created opportunities, it has also widened the gap between the wealthy and the less fortunate. The benefits haven't been evenly distributed, creating a social imbalance that needs careful attention.

Brain Drain Threatens: The departure of skilled workers seeking greener pastures abroad can lead to a "brain drain," depriving Sindh of vital talent and expertise. It's like losing key dancers from the ensemble.

Sindhi Entrepreneurs: The Agile Choreographers

Sindhi entrepreneurs and businesses are the creative choreographers of this globalization dance. Their ability to adapt, innovate, and compete determines the success of the performance.

Embracing Technology's Rhythm: Sindhi entrepreneurs are harnessing the power of technology, using e-commerce, digital marketing, and online payment systems to reach new customers and expand their businesses. They're incorporating modern moves into their traditional dance.

Global Partnerships: A Harmonious Duet: Many Sindhi businesses are forming partnerships with international companies, gaining access to new markets, technologies, and expertise. It's like a beautiful duet, combining strengths and creating a more powerful performance.

Niche Markets: A Unique Solo: Some entrepreneurs are focusing on niche markets where their unique cultural heritage and strengths shine. This is their solo performance, captivating audiences with their individuality.

Sustainability: Dancing in Harmony with Nature: A growing number of businesses are embracing sustainability, adopting eco-friendly practices, and supporting local communities. They're ensuring the dance is not just beautiful but also responsible and enduring.

Traditional Livelihoods: Preserving the Heritage

Globalization's impact on traditional livelihoods is a complex dance step, with both preservation and adaptation.

Agriculture: Adapting to New Tastes: Sindh's agriculture sector, the backbone of many livelihoods, faces challenges from imported products and changing consumer preferences. Farmers need to adapt, perhaps by exploring organic farming or specializing in unique local produce.

Handicrafts: Keeping the Tradition Alive: The intricate beauty of Sindhi handicrafts faces competition from mass-produced goods. Artisans need support in marketing their authentic creations and preserving their invaluable skills for future generations.

Cultural Tourism: Sharing the Story: Globalization has opened doors for cultural tourism, offering a stage to showcase Sindh's rich history and heritage. This brings economic benefits and creates opportunities to share the province's unique story with the world.

Practical Steps: Ensuring a Graceful Performance

To ensure everyone benefits from this globalization dance, Sindh needs to take proactive steps:

Capacity Building: Strengthening the Dancers: Providing training and support to local businesses and artisans equips them with the skills and knowledge to thrive in the global market. It's like providing rigorous dance lessons to refine their technique.

Market Access: Expanding the Stage: Facilitating access to global markets helps Sindhi products reach wider audiences. This could involve organizing trade fairs, creating online platforms, and connecting with international buyers. It's like securing bigger, more prestigious venues for the performance.

Financial Inclusion: Funding the Dream: Access to finance is crucial for small businesses and artisans to grow and innovate. Microfinance institutions and government loan schemes can provide the necessary support. It's like providing costumes and resources to help the dancers shine.

Cultural Preservation: Honoring the Roots: Promoting and preserving traditional crafts and cultural heritage keeps Sindh's identity strong and attracts cultural tourism. It's like cherishing the traditional dance forms that make the performance unique and meaningful.

The Final Bow

Globalization presents a complex choreography for Sindh. By embracing innovation, promoting sustainability, and supporting local businesses and traditional crafts, Sindh can dance gracefully on the world stage, reaping the rewards while preserving its unique identity.

Subtopic 3: Preserving Values: Safeguarding Cultural Heritage in a Changing World

Introduction

In a world that's constantly evolving, holding onto the traditions and customs that make us unique is like trying to catch smoke. Globalization and modernization are powerful forces, and they often sweep aside the beautiful tapestry of cultures that have developed over centuries. We risk losing the vibrant threads of languages, the intricate patterns of ancient customs, and the rich hues of traditional values. But cultural heritage is the soul of a community, its living memory. It's the bridge that connects us to our ancestors and the foundation upon which future generations build their identity.

This subtopic delves into the challenges of safeguarding our cultural heritage in the face of these relentless forces. We'll explore how education, families, and communities can act as guardians of tradition, passing the torch of cultural knowledge to younger generations. We'll also examine how cultural tourism, when done responsibly, can be a powerful tool for both preserving and celebrating our cultural treasures. Finally, we'll brainstorm practical ideas for educational programs and community initiatives that can ignite cultural awareness and spark meaningful conversations across generations.

Challenges in a Shifting Landscape

Globalization and modernization have brought the world closer together, but this interconnectedness comes at a cost. Here are some of the hurdles we face in preserving our cultural heritage:

Cultural Homogenization: Like a powerful wave, Western culture often washes over traditional practices, leading to a worrying sameness. Imagine a world where everyone wears the same clothes, listens to the same music, and eats the same food – a world stripped of its vibrant cultural diversity.

The Fading Echo of Languages: As global languages like English dominate, the whispers of ancient tongues grow fainter. With the loss of each language, a whole universe of stories, songs, and cultural knowledge vanishes.

Culture Turned Commodity: In the pursuit of profit, cultural heritage can be packaged and sold like any other product. Imagine a sacred dance performed not for its spiritual significance but for the entertainment of tourists. This commodification can strip cultural practices of their true meaning.

Cultural Appropriation: Borrowing elements from another culture without understanding or respect is like taking a beautiful melody and playing it out of tune. It can distort the original meaning and cause deep offense.

The Uprooted Tree: Urbanization and migration can sever the roots that connect people to their ancestral lands and traditions. Imagine a tree transplanted to a foreign soil, struggling to survive in an unfamiliar environment.

Guardians of Tradition: Education, Family, and Community

Despite these challenges, hope remains. We have the power to be the guardians of our cultural heritage:

Formal Education: Schools can be vibrant centers for cultural learning, where children discover the stories, songs, and dances of their ancestors. Imagine classrooms transformed into time machines, transporting students to the past.

Family Ties: Families are the heart of cultural transmission. Parents and grandparents can share their memories, recipes, and traditions, weaving a rich tapestry of cultural knowledge for their children. Imagine a family gathered around a fireplace, listening to stories passed down through generations.

Community Spirit: Communities can host festivals, workshops, and gatherings that celebrate their unique cultural identity. Imagine a village coming alive with the rhythm of drums, the swirl of colorful costumes, and the joyous laughter of people connected by their shared heritage.

Cultural Tourism: A Double-Edged Sword

Cultural tourism can be a powerful force for good, bringing economic benefits to communities and fostering cultural understanding Imagine travelers exploring ancient ruins, learning traditional crafts, or participating in local ceremonies. However, it's crucial to ensure that tourism doesn't erode the very culture it seeks to showcase. Responsible tourism involves:

Respectful Engagement: Tourists should approach cultural experiences with humility and a willingness to learn.

Community Involvement: Local communities should have a voice in how their culture is presented and benefit directly from tourism revenue.

Sustainability: Tourism should be managed in a way that protects the environment and preserves cultural sites for future generations.

Practical Applications: Fanning the Flames of Cultural Awareness

Here are some practical ways to promote cultural awareness and encourage intergenerational dialogue:

Living Museums: Create interactive exhibits and workshops where visitors can experience traditional crafts, music, and storytelling firsthand.
Cultural Exchanges: Organize programs where people from different cultures can share their traditions and learn from one another.

Oral History Projects: Record the stories and memories of elders to preserve valuable cultural knowledge for future generations.
Digital Archives: Create online platforms to showcase cultural heritage through videos, photos, and audio recordings.

Conclusion

Preserving our cultural heritage is a shared responsibility. By working together, we can ensure that the flame of tradition continues to burn brightly, illuminating the path for generations to come. Let's embrace our cultural diversity, celebrate our shared humanity, and protect the precious legacy of our ancestors.

Subtopic 4: Cultural Resilience: Adapting and Thriving in a Globalized World

Introduction

In today's interconnected world, cultures are constantly interacting and evolving. While some struggle to maintain their unique identity amidst the influx of global trends, others, like the Sindhi culture, exhibit remarkable resilience. This resilience stems from their ability to adapt, innovate, and leverage technology to connect with Sindhi communities worldwide.

Analyzing the Resilience of Sindhi Culture in the Face of Globalization

The Sindhi people, with their roots in the Sindh region of Pakistan, possess a vibrant culture encompassing language, religion, music, dance, and literature. While globalization has posed challenges to the preservation of their cultural heritage, the Sindhi people have demonstrated remarkable resilience.

One key factor contributing to this resilience is their adaptability. Sindhis have skillfully integrated elements of Western culture into their own, enriching their traditions without compromising their identity. Furthermore, they have successfully adapted their traditional industries to meet the demands of the modern world.

Another crucial aspect of Sindhi cultural resilience lies in their innovation and creativity. Sindhi artists, writers, and musicians continuously produce new works that reflect contemporary issues and resonate with younger generations. This ongoing cultural innovation ensures that Sindhi culture remains relevant and engaging.

Finally, technology and social media have played a pivotal role in connecting Sindhi communities across the globe. Through platforms like Facebook, Twitter, and Instagram, Sindhis can share their culture, experiences, and traditions, fostering a sense of unity and preserving their cultural identity.

Exploring the Role of Cultural Innovation and Creativity in Maintaining Cultural Relevance and Engaging Younger Generations

Cultural innovation and creativity are vital for ensuring that Sindhi culture remains relevant and captivates the interest of younger generations. Sindhi artists, writers, and musicians play a crucial role in this endeavor by creating works that reflect contemporary issues and appeal to younger audiences.

For instance, renowned Sindhi musician Sajjad Ali masterfully blends traditional Sindhi music with Western influences, creating a unique sound that resonates with both young and old. Similarly, Sindhi writer Jumma Khan tackles contemporary issues in his novels and short stories, sparking thought-provoking discussions and engaging younger readers.

In the realm of dance, Kiran Shah has pioneered a new style that combines traditional Sindhi dance with contemporary techniques, captivating audiences with visually stunning and captivating performances.

These innovative artists, along with many others, help ensure that Sindhi culture remains vibrant and relevant for younger generations.

Investigating the Potential of Technology and Social Media to Promote Cultural Exchange and Connect Sindhi Communities Across the Globe

Technology and social media have immense potential to promote cultural exchange and connect Sindhi communities worldwide. Sindhi diaspora communities utilize platforms like Facebook, Twitter, and Instagram to connect, share their culture, and stay connected to their roots.

Sindhi cultural organizations also leverage technology to promote cultural exchange. The Sindhi Heritage Foundation, for example, has created a website and social media presence to share information about Sindhi culture and history, promote events, and connect with Sindhi communities globally.

By harnessing the power of technology and social media, Sindhi communities can maintain their cultural identity, connect with each other, and share their rich heritage with a broader audience.

Practical Application: Supporting Cultural Initiatives that Foster Creativity, Innovation, and Cultural Exchange Among Sindhi Communities

To further support Sindhi cultural resilience, several practical steps can be taken:

Financial Support: Provide financial assistance to Sindhi artists, writers, and musicians to enable them to continue their creative endeavors.
Showcase Opportunities: Create platforms and events for Sindhi artists, writers, and musicians to showcase their work to a wider audience.

Organizational Support: Support the development and growth of Sindhi cultural organizations that promote cultural preservation and exchange.

Technology Utilization: Encourage the use of technology and social media to connect Sindhi communities worldwide and facilitate cultural exchange.

By actively supporting these initiatives, we can contribute to the continued flourishing of Sindhi culture in the face of globalization.

Conclusion

Sindhi culture has demonstrated remarkable resilience in navigating the challenges of globalization. This resilience is rooted in their adaptability, innovation, and effective use of technology to connect with Sindhi communities worldwide.

By continuing to support cultural initiatives that foster creativity, innovation, and cultural exchange, we can help ensure that Sindhi culture thrives for generations to come.

The Global Sindhi: Diaspora Communities and the Quest for Belonging

Imagine a vibrant tapestry woven with threads of resilience, entrepreneurship, and cultural richness. This is the story of the Sindhi diaspora, a global community with roots tracing back to the ancient Indus River Valley.

A Journey Through Time:

For centuries, Sindhi traders and artisans, driven by an adventurous spirit, sailed across oceans and traversed land routes, carrying their culture and skills to distant shores. Then came the tumultuous partition of India in 1947, forcing a mass exodus of Sindhi Hindus and Sikhs. Imagine families leaving behind their ancestral homes, carrying little more than hope and a determination to rebuild their lives. This wave of migration scattered Sindhis across the globe, planting seeds that would blossom into vibrant communities.

A Global Mosaic:

Today, Sindhi communities thrive in bustling metropolises and quiet suburbs, from the vibrant streets of Mumbai to the multicultural neighborhoods of London and New York. Picture bustling Sindhi markets filled with the aroma of fragrant spices and the sounds of lively bargaining, or community centers resonating with the melodies of traditional Sindhi music and the rhythmic beats of their energetic dances.

More Than Survivors:

Sindhis are not just defined by their history. They are entrepreneurs, doctors, artists, and educators. They are renowned for their business acumen, their love of education, and their unwavering commitment to family and community. Imagine a Sindhi family gathering, generations sharing stories and laughter, their resilience and optimism a testament to their enduring spirit.

Connecting the Dots:

Now, imagine an interactive online map that brings this vibrant diaspora to life. Click on a city and discover the unique story of its Sindhi community. See their journey through historical photos and personal narratives. Explore their cultural traditions through music, dance, and cuisine. This map becomes a bridge, connecting Sindhis across continents, fostering a sense of shared identity and preserving their rich heritage for future generations.

A Case Study in Success: Sindhis in the USA

Zoom in on the United States, and you'll find a thriving Sindhi community that has woven itself into the fabric of American society. From the early immigrants who arrived with dreams of a better future to the successful entrepreneurs and professionals of today, Sindhis have made significant contributions to their adopted homeland. Picture a Sindhi American youth, confidently navigating both their heritage and their American identity, a testament to the community's successful integration.

The Sindhi story is one of resilience, adaptation, and success. It's a story that deserves to be told, explored, and celebrated.

Subtopic 2: Cultural Transmission: Preserving Heritage Across Borders

Imagine the aroma of cardamom and cloves swirling in the air as young Anika, her eyes sparkling with excitement, carefully folds delicate samosas alongside her grandmother in their London kitchen. This isn't just cooking; it's a ritual, a passing of the torch. Anika's grandmother, with her weathered hands and a voice tinged with the melody of her homeland, Sindh, shares stories of bustling markets in Karachi, where the scent of spices hung heavy in the air and laughter echoed through the narrow streets. This is how Sindhi culture survives, one generation whispering its secrets to the next, even thousands of miles away from the Indus River.

The Sindhi diaspora, scattered like seeds on the wind, faces the constant challenge of nurturing their roots in foreign soil. It's a delicate dance, balancing assimilation with preservation, honoring the past while embracing the present. But the Sindhi people are resilient, their spirit woven from the same vibrant threads as their intricate embroidery.

In the heart of London, a vibrant community center pulsates with life. Here, the Sindhi language, a song almost lost to the whispers of time, finds new voice. Children, their eyes wide with curiosity, trace the elegant curves of the Sindhi script, their laughter mingling with the rhythmic beats of a traditional dholak drum. This is the Sindhi Heritage Center, a haven where elders share their wisdom, artists showcase their talents, and the aroma of biryani and sai bhaji fills the air, a fragrant reminder of home.

But preserving heritage isn't confined to the walls of community centers. It thrives in the online world, where social media groups buzz with discussions in Sindhi, connecting families separated by continents. It lives in the music of artists like Saif Samejo, whose soulful voice blends traditional Sindhi folk with modern influences, creating a bridge between generations. And it flourishes in the kitchens of families like Anika's, where recipes passed down through generations become a love language, a tangible connection to a homeland that exists both in memory and on the plate.

Of course, the journey isn't without its challenges. The allure of the dominant culture can be strong, tempting young Sindhis to shed their traditions like an outgrown garment. Intermarriage, while a beautiful tapestry of cultures, can sometimes dilute the vibrancy of Sindhi customs. And the geographical distance from Sindh can ache like a persistent longing, a yearning for the familiar sights, sounds, and smells of home.

Yet, the Sindhi spirit perseveres. Like the mighty Indus River that carved its way through ancient lands, Sindhi culture flows through the veins of its people, adapting, evolving, and finding new ways to express itself. From the bustling streets of London to the quiet suburbs of New York, the flame of Sindhi heritage burns bright, fueled by the love, resilience, and unwavering spirit of its people.

What can we do to help fan these flames? Support Sindhi cultural centers, celebrate Sindhi festivals, learn a few phrases of the Sindhi language, and listen to the stories of the elders. For in preserving the heritage of the Sindhi diaspora, we enrich the tapestry of our global community.

Imagine a vibrant tapestry woven with threads from across the globe, each thread representing a Sindhi community, connected and interwoven. This is the picture of the Sindhi diaspora, a people scattered yet united by their shared heritage. But how do they maintain this connection across continents? The answer lies in a dynamic blend of tradition and technology.

Think of community organizations as bustling marketplaces, filled with the aroma of traditional Sindhi cuisine, the sounds of lively music, and the vibrant colors of cultural dress. These are places where generations converge, sharing stories, celebrating festivals, and passing the torch of their heritage to the young. Organizations like the Sindhi Association of North America and the World Sindhi Congress act as the central squares of these marketplaces, where Sindhis find belonging and keep their traditions alive.

Then picture cultural centers as museums and libraries, safeguarding the treasures of Sindhi history. They're not just dusty archives, though. They pulse with the rhythm of dance classes, resonate with the melodies of language lessons, and showcase the intricate beauty of traditional crafts. Places like the Sindhi Cultural Center in Dubai and the Institute of Sindhology in Pakistan are the keepers of the Sindhi story, ensuring it's not forgotten.

Now, enter the digital age. Imagine a network of glowing pathways connecting every Sindhi, no matter where they are. Social media groups become virtual "chai khanas" where people share news, laughter, and support in real-time. Websites like Sindhi Sangat transform into online "baithaks," offering a wealth of information and connecting individuals eager to learn and connect. 1 Virtual events, from lively dance performances to soul-stirring religious gatherings, bring the community together in a digital embrace.

This blend of physical and virtual spaces creates a powerful synergy. It allows for a vibrant exchange of culture, ensuring traditions are not only preserved but also evolve and adapt in a globalized world. It provides a safety net, offering support and resources to those navigating new environments. Most importantly, it empowers Sindhis to define and celebrate their identity on their own terms.

Globalization and technology haven't just connected the Sindhi diaspora; they've transformed it. The ease of communication has strengthened bonds, while exposure to new cultures has led to a beautiful hybridization of traditions. The accessibility of information has shifted power dynamics, giving individuals a greater voice in shaping their community's narrative.

To further empower this digital renaissance, we need to focus on creating user-friendly platforms that cater to the diverse needs of the community. Imagine vibrant online spaces filled with engaging content: interactive language courses, virtual museum tours, and immersive cultural experiences. By fostering collaboration between tech experts and community leaders, we can build a digital ecosystem that is both powerful and accessible.

The Sindhi diaspora is a testament to the resilience of culture and the power of connection. By investing in online platforms and digital resources, we can help ensure that this vibrant tapestry continues to weave its magic across continents, for generations to come.

Home and Belonging: A Tapestry Woven Across the Globe

A Tale of Two Worlds

Imagine a young Sindhi woman, born and raised in the heart of London. As she sips her morning chai, the aroma of cardamom and cloves fills her senses, transporting her to the bustling bazaars of Karachi. This is the paradox of the Sindhi diaspora: a people bound by shared heritage, yet scattered across the globe.

The Weight of History

The Sindhi diaspora, a tapestry woven with threads of history, culture, and migration, is a testament to the human spirit's resilience. Forced displacement, political turmoil, and economic hardship have shaped the destinies of countless Sindhis. Yet, even in the face of adversity, their cultural identity has endured.

A Sense of Place, A Sense of Self

For many Sindhi, the concept of "home" is a complex and ever-evolving notion. It is a place of origin, a place of memory, and a place of belonging. It is the bustling streets of Hyderabad, the serene landscapes of Thatta, and the warm embrace of family and friends.

But home is also wherever Sindhis find themselves, whether it's the vibrant metropolis of New York, the tranquil countryside of Australia, or the bustling markets of Dubai. It is the shared experiences, the common language, and the enduring traditions that bind them together.

The Power of Memory

Memory is the cornerstone of cultural identity. It is the thread that connects past, present, and future. For Sindhis, oral traditions, folklore, and music have been instrumental in preserving their heritage. These stories, songs, and dances are passed down from generation to generation, keeping the spirit of Sindh alive.

A Digital Diaspora

In recent years, the internet has revolutionized the way Sindhis connect with their heritage. Online forums, social media groups, and virtual communities have emerged, providing a platform for sharing stories, recipes, and cultural practices. This digital diaspora has fostered a sense of global community, transcending geographical boundaries.

The Future of the Sindhi Diaspora

As the world becomes increasingly interconnected, the future of the Sindhi diaspora is uncertain. However, one thing is certain: the enduring spirit of the Sindhi people will continue to shape their destiny. By embracing their heritage, adapting to new challenges, and forging new connections, the Sindhi diaspora will continue to thrive.

Documenting the Past, Shaping the Future

To understand the complexities of the Sindhi diaspora, it is essential to document their experiences through oral history projects and ethnographic research. By listening to the stories of individuals and communities, we can gain valuable insights into their lives, their struggles, and their hopes for the future.

Through these efforts, we can ensure that the rich cultural heritage of the Sindhi people is preserved for generations to come.

Education as a Lifeline: Preserving Sindhi Language and Culture in the Classroom

Breathing Life into Sindhi: A Tapestry of Language and Learning

Imagine a vibrant tapestry, woven with threads of history, culture, and identity. This is the Sindhi language, spoken by millions in Pakistan and India. But this tapestry is fading, its intricate patterns obscured by challenges in education. Let's explore how we can revitalize Sindhi, ensuring it thrives for generations to come.

Primary Schools: Nurturing the Seeds of Language

Imagine young children, their eyes bright with curiosity, eager to learn. Yet, many Sindhi schools lack the resources to nurture this enthusiasm. Classrooms are overcrowded, textbooks outdated, and teachers struggle with limited training. This is where the seeds of language are sown, and they need fertile ground to grow.

Embracing Technology: Imagine interactive whiteboards bringing Sindhi folktales to life, language learning apps turning grammar into engaging games, and online platforms connecting students with pen pals across the globe.

Celebrating Culture: Imagine classrooms transformed into vibrant cultural hubs, with storytelling sessions by local elders, traditional Sindhi music echoing through the halls, and colorful handicrafts showcasing the beauty of Sindhi art.

Empowering Teachers: Imagine passionate teachers equipped with the latest pedagogical tools, attending workshops led by experts in language acquisition, and collaborating to create engaging Sindhi curriculum.

Universities: Igniting the Flame of Scholarship

Imagine university halls buzzing with intellectual curiosity, yet Sindhi language programs struggle to attract students. The allure of "practical" subjects like science and business overshadows the richness of language and literature. It's time to reignite the flame of scholarship and showcase the diverse career paths a Sindhi degree can unlock.

Bridging the Gap: Imagine Sindhi language graduates finding fulfilling roles as journalists, translators, cultural ambassadors, and educators, their skills bridging communities and fostering understanding.

Research and Revival: Imagine research grants supporting the exploration of Sindhi literature, linguistics, and history, leading to the publication of new textbooks, dictionaries, and academic journals.

Creative Collaborations: Imagine partnerships between universities and cultural institutions, leading to the creation of Sindhi theater productions, film festivals, and literary conferences, showcasing the language's versatility.

Innovative Approaches: Weaving a Richer Tapestry

Imagine a future where Sindhi thrives, woven into the fabric of society. This requires a multifaceted approach, embracing innovation and celebrating diversity.

Immersion Programs: Imagine young children immersed in a world of Sindhi, learning through songs, games, and storytelling, developing fluency effortlessly.

Bilingual Education: Imagine students seamlessly navigating between Sindhi and other languages, their minds enriched by diverse perspectives and cultural understanding.

Heritage Language Programs: Imagine individuals reconnecting with their Sindhi roots, discovering their heritage through language classes, cultural workshops, and community events.

Challenges and Opportunities: Embracing the Future

The path to revitalizing Sindhi is not without its challenges. Limited resources, political complexities, and societal pressures all play a role. Yet, within these challenges lie opportunities for growth and innovation.

By embracing technology, celebrating culture, empowering teachers, and fostering collaboration, we can create a vibrant future for Sindhi. Let's work together to ensure this beautiful tapestry continues to enrich our world.

Let's embark on a journey to the heart of Sindhi language learning, where tradition meets innovation, and passion ignites discovery.

Meet Fatima, a teacher with a twinkle in her eye and a love for her mother tongue that burns bright. She yearns to share this passion with her students, but the old textbooks and rote learning methods seem to stifle their enthusiasm. One day, she stumbles upon a treasure trove of innovative teaching techniques, and her classroom is forever transformed.

Imagine:

A bustling marketplace erupts in Fatima's classroom. Shy Kiran, usually hesitant to speak, confidently orders "aloo tuk" (potato fritters) in fluent Sindhi, her face beaming with pride. Energetic Asif, once a grammar-phobe, now passionately barters for a lower price, his eyes sparkling with mischief. This is Communicative Language Teaching (CLT) in action, where real-life scenarios bring the language to life.

The classroom walls dissolve, and students find themselves transported to the vibrant colors and rhythmic beats of a Sindhi cultural festival. They work together, piecing together the story of this celebration through online research, interviews with local musicians, and vibrant photographs. This is Task-Based Language Teaching (TBLT), where learning becomes an adventure, a collaborative quest for knowledge.

History books spring open, revealing the secrets of the ancient Indus Valley Civilization. Students decipher Sindhi inscriptions on clay tablets, their fingers tracing the echoes of a bygone era. They debate the significance of archaeological discoveries, their voices weaving a tapestry of past and present. This is Content and Language Integrated Learning (CLIL), where language becomes a key to unlock the mysteries of the world.

A digital playground emerges, filled with interactive games, colorful challenges, and virtual rewards. Students race against the clock to complete Sindhi vocabulary quizzes, their fingers flying across touchscreens. They earn badges for mastering grammar rules, their laughter echoing through the classroom. This is gamification, where learning is infused with the thrill of play and the joy of achievement.

The classroom is flipped! At home, students delve into the intricacies of Sindhi grammar through engaging online videos and interactive exercises. In class, they become active explorers, debating grammatical nuances, solving linguistic puzzles, and collaborating on creative projects.

Fatima, now a facilitator and guide, witnesses a newfound spark of curiosity in her students' eyes.

But the magic doesn't stop there. Fatima introduces her students to the soul of the Sindhi language:

They lose themselves in the verses of Shah Abdul Latif Bhittai's poetry, their hearts resonating with the Sufi mystic's timeless wisdom.

They tap their feet to the infectious rhythm of a Sufi qawwali, their bodies swaying to the melodies that have echoed through Sindh for centuries.

They are captivated by the stories of brave warriors and mythical creatures in Sindhi folktales, their imaginations soaring on the wings of ancient legends.

They watch classic Sindhi films, their eyes glued to the screen as they navigate the nuances of dialogue and cultural expression.

Through these authentic materials, the Sindhi language becomes more than just words and grammar; it becomes a gateway to a rich cultural heritage, a vibrant tapestry of stories, music, and art.

Fatima, empowered by these innovative approaches, becomes more than just a teacher; she becomes a guide, a mentor, and a fellow traveler on a journey of linguistic and cultural discovery. Her classroom is no longer a place of passive learning, but a vibrant hub of exploration, collaboration, and joyful expression.

This is the future of Sindhi language learning: a future where technology and tradition dance hand in hand, where innovation sparks passion, and where every student has the opportunity to embrace the beauty and richness of this ancient tongue.

Join the movement! Explore the resources, connect with online communities, and become a champion for Sindhi language and culture. Together, we can ensure that this vibrant heritage continues to thrive for generations to come.

Sindhi Language Curriculum

1. Immersive Cultural Experiences

Virtual Field Trips: Use virtual reality to transport students to historical sites like Mohenjo-daro, the bustling markets of Hyderabad, or the serene landscapes of Thatta.

Cultural Exchange Programs: Facilitate virtual exchanges with Sindhi-speaking communities around the world. Students can engage in discussions, share stories, and practice their language skills.

Community Engagement: Organize cultural events like poetry slams, music performances, and art exhibitions to connect students with their heritage and the wider community.

Heritage Crafts Workshops: Introduce students to traditional crafts like Ajrak dyeing, pottery, and embroidery. These hands-on activities can deepen their understanding of Sindhi culture.

2. Storytelling and Creative Expression

Oral History Projects: Encourage students to interview elders in the community to record their personal stories and experiences.

Creative Writing Workshops: Inspire students to write short stories, poems, and plays in Sindhi.

Filmmaking: Guide students in creating short films that explore themes from Sindhi history, literature, and folklore.

Music and Dance: Introduce students to traditional Sindhi music and dance forms.

3. Interdisciplinary Learning

History and Language: Connect historical events with the evolution of the Sindhi language.

Literature and Language: Analyze classic Sindhi literature to understand the nuances of the language.

Art and Language: Explore the visual language of Sindhi art, including miniature paintings and calligraphy.

Science and Language: Discuss scientific concepts in Sindhi to enhance vocabulary and comprehension.

4. Technology-Enhanced Learning

Language Learning Apps: Utilize language learning apps to make practice fun and engaging.

Gamification: Create language games and quizzes to motivate students.

Online Forums: Foster online communities where students can discuss language and cultural topics.

AI-Powered Language Tools: Use AI tools for personalized language feedback and translation.

5. Experiential Learning

Cultural Festivals: Organize festivals celebrating Sindhi culture, including food, music, dance, and traditional games.

Cooking Classes: Teach students to cook traditional Sindhi dishes, connecting language with culinary arts.

Nature Walks: Explore local natural sites and discuss their significance in Sindhi folklore and poetry.

Volunteer Opportunities: Encourage students to volunteer at local organizations to give back to the community and practice their language skills.

By implementing these strategies, we can create a vibrant and dynamic Sindhi language curriculum that fosters cultural pride, critical thinking, and a lifelong love of learning.

Subtopic 4: Keeping Sindhi Alive: A Lifelong Journey of Language and Culture

Introduction

Imagine a vibrant tapestry woven with threads of language, stories, music, and dance – this is the cultural heritage of the Sindhi people. While schools lay the foundation, it's the lifelong journey of learning and connection that truly keeps this tapestry alive. This section explores how we can inspire a love for Sindhi language and culture that extends far beyond the classroom walls.

Why Embrace Sindhi Throughout Life?

Think of it like this:

A Treasure Chest of Heritage: Each generation holds the key to passing down the treasures of Sindhi language and culture. Lifelong learning ensures these treasures aren't lost to time.

The Heart of a Community: When people share a language and cultural heritage, they form a strong, interconnected community. Continued engagement strengthens those bonds and creates a sense of belonging.

Unlocking Your Mind: Learning Sindhi is like opening a secret door in your mind! It boosts your brainpower, helps you solve problems in new ways, and sparks your creativity.

A World of Understanding: By immersing ourselves in Sindhi language and culture, we gain a deeper appreciation for the diverse tapestry of human experience. This fosters empathy and respect for others.

Open Doors to Opportunity: In a globalized world, knowing Sindhi can open doors to new connections, careers, and entrepreneurial ventures, particularly within the Sindhi community.

Creating Spaces for Sindhi to Flourish

Here's how we can make lifelong learning a reality:

Community Hubs: Imagine lively community centers, libraries, and schools buzzing with Sindhi language classes, workshops, and cultural gatherings. These spaces become vibrant hubs where people of all ages can connect and learn together.

Celebrations of Culture: Picture colorful festivals, captivating workshops, thought-provoking seminars, and soul-stirring concerts that bring Sindhi culture to life. These events create unforgettable experiences and foster a shared sense of identity.

The Digital World: From interactive websites and engaging blogs to captivating podcasts and videos, online resources offer a wealth of Sindhi language learning materials and cultural content, accessible to anyone, anywhere.

Bridging Generations: Imagine young people learning the art of storytelling from their grandparents, or discovering traditional recipes passed down through generations. Intergenerational learning and mentorship programs create beautiful connections between young and old, ensuring that cultural knowledge is cherished and preserved.

The Magic of Intergenerational Learning

Imagine a young person sitting beside an elder, listening to captivating stories of their ancestors, learning the nuances of Sindhi proverbs, and absorbing the wisdom of a lifetime. Intergenerational learning is a powerful way to bridge the generation gap and ensure that cultural knowledge is passed on with love and respect.

Bringing it to Life: Building Programs That Inspire

Creating successful community-based language programs and cultural events requires a collaborative spirit and a touch of magic:

Listen to the Community: Understand their dreams, needs, and interests to create programs and events that truly resonate.

Gather Support: Secure funding, resources, and partnerships to make these initiatives sustainable and impactful.

Passionate Guides: Recruit experienced and enthusiastic instructors and volunteers who can ignite a love for Sindhi in others.

Spread the Word: Promote these programs with creativity and enthusiasm, inviting everyone to join the journey of lifelong learning.

Success Stories: Inspiration in Action

Let's draw inspiration from those who have paved the way:

The Sindhi Language Institute (SLI): A beacon of language and culture, offering a rich tapestry of programs that connect Sindhi people across North America.

The Sindhi Cultural Society of North America (SCSNA): A vibrant hub of cultural celebrations, fostering a sense of community and providing valuable support for students exploring Sindhi heritage.

The Sindhi Heritage Foundation (SHF): A guardian of Sindhi language, literature, and culture, ensuring that its treasures are preserved for generations to come.

Conclusion

Lifelong learning is the heartbeat of a thriving Sindhi community. By nurturing a love for Sindhi language and culture, we weave a vibrant tapestry that connects generations and celebrates a rich heritage. Let's work together to create a future where Sindhi continues to flourish, enriching the lives of all who embrace it.

Environmental Stewardship: Protecting the Land and People of Sindh

The Scorched Earth: Sindh's Struggle for Survival in a Changing Climate

In the heart of Pakistan, where the Indus River snakes its way to the Arabian Sea, lies Sindh, a land of ancient civilizations and vibrant cultures. But today, Sindh faces a formidable foe: climate change. This isn't just about rising temperatures; it's about livelihoods lost, traditions threatened, and a battle for survival against the relentless forces of nature.

Imagine a land where the sun beats down with an unforgiving intensity, where once-fertile fields are now parched and cracked, and where the sea encroaches upon the land, swallowing homes and livelihoods. This is the reality for the people of Sindh, who are on the frontlines of climate change.

A Symphony of Disruptions

The changing climate has unleashed a symphony of disruptions in Sindh. Rising temperatures have turned the province into a furnace, with heatwaves becoming more frequent and intense. The life-giving monsoon rains, once a source of hope and abundance, are now erratic and unpredictable, bringing devastating floods one year and crippling droughts the next.

The sea, once a source of sustenance and trade, is now a menacing force, its rising levels threatening to inundate coastal communities and salinate precious freshwater resources. And as if this wasn't enough, extreme weather events, like cyclones and storms, are becoming more frequent and ferocious, leaving a trail of destruction in their wake.

Vulnerability on Many Fronts

The impacts of climate change are not felt equally in Sindh. Coastal communities, dependent on fishing and tourism, are watching their livelihoods disappear beneath the waves. Farmers, the backbone of Sindh's economy, are struggling to cope with erratic rainfall and water scarcity. And the poorest of the poor, those living in makeshift shelters and lacking basic amenities, are the most vulnerable to the ravages of extreme weather.

The province's rich biodiversity is also under threat. Mangrove forests, the guardians of the coast, are being eroded by rising sea levels and saltwater intrusion. Wetlands, havens for wildlife and vital for water storage, are drying up. And forests, the lungs of the planet, are shrinking, their ability to absorb carbon dioxide diminishing.

Seeds of Resilience

But amidst this grim reality, there are seeds of resilience. Communities are coming together to adapt to the changing climate. Farmers are adopting water-efficient irrigation techniques and planting drought-resistant crops. Coastal communities are building seawalls and restoring mangrove forests to protect their homes and livelihoods.

The government is investing in early warning systems and disaster preparedness measures to reduce the impact of extreme weather events. And there is a growing recognition of the importance of sustainable practices, such as renewable energy, energy efficiency, and waste reduction, to mitigate climate change and build a more sustainable future.

A Call for Collective Action

The challenges facing Sindh are immense, but they are not insurmountable. The province needs continued investment in adaptation measures and sustainable practices. It needs support from the international community to address the impacts of climate change. And it needs the collective will of its people to build a more resilient and sustainable future.

The story of Sindh is a story of resilience, of communities adapting to a changing climate and fighting for their survival. It is a story that resonates with people around the world who are facing similar challenges. And it is a story that reminds us that we are all connected and that we must work together to protect our planet and build a more sustainable future for all.

The Indus River, the lifeblood of Pakistan, is drying up. Like a withering artery, its flow weakens, leaving the people of Sindh, at the river's end, parched and desperate. This isn't just about dry taps and wilting crops; it's about families struggling to survive, children falling ill from polluted water, and the very fabric of a community fraying at the edges.

Imagine a farmer in Sindh, his brow furrowed as he stares at cracked earth. The once-fertile land, inherited from his forefathers, now yields a meager harvest. His children, their bellies swollen from waterborne diseases, cry out for relief. This is the reality of Sindh's water crisis, a crisis fueled by a dwindling Indus, a thirsty population, and the relentless exploitation of groundwater.

The Indus Water Treaty, meant to ensure equitable sharing between India and Pakistan, has become a source of contention, adding another layer of complexity to Sindh's woes. Disputes over dams and water allocation leave Sindh feeling like a forgotten child, its needs cast aside in a political tug-of-war.

But amidst the despair, there's a flicker of hope. Communities are coming together, like parched seedlings seeking solace in shared roots. They're learning to harvest rainwater, embracing water-efficient farming techniques, and becoming stewards of their precious resource.

This isn't just a story of scarcity; it's a story of resilience. It's about the ingenuity of a people determined to survive, to adapt, and to reclaim their future. It's about the power of collective action, where every drop saved, every well protected, is a victory against the encroaching desert.

Sindh's water crisis is a wake-up call, a stark reminder of our interconnectedness with nature. It's a call to action, urging us to protect our rivers, conserve our groundwater, and ensure access to clean water for all. For in the fight for water, we're fighting for life itself.

Sindh's Silent Struggle: A Story of Pollution and Hope

Imagine a land where the air hangs heavy with unseen threats, where the life-giving waters are tainted, and the very soil beneath your feet carries the burden of toxins. This is the reality for many in Sindh, a province in Pakistan grappling with a silent struggle against environmental pollution.

A Choking Reality:

The bustling streets of Sindh's cities are choked with vehicles, many old and coughing out fumes, filling the air with a noxious cocktail of pollutants. Factories hum with activity, but their chimneys also spew out harmful gases, adding to the invisible burden in the air. Even the simple act of burning waste, a common practice, releases a wave of harmful particles into the atmosphere. This polluted air seeps into homes and lungs, causing a rise in respiratory illnesses, heart problems, and even premature deaths. Children, with their developing lungs, and the elderly, with their weakened bodies, are particularly vulnerable.

Poisoned Waters:

The Indus River, the lifeblood of Sindh, is under siege. Untreated waste from factories flows freely into its waters, while agricultural runoff carries with it a toxic mix of pesticides and fertilizers. Even the very ground beneath Sindh is contaminated, with industrial waste and improper disposal of hazardous materials poisoning the soil. This contamination has far-reaching consequences, impacting not only the health of the people but also the delicate balance of the ecosystem.

The Fight for a Healthier Future:

Despite these challenges, there is hope. The Sindh Environmental Protection Agency (SEPA) is working tirelessly to implement regulations and control industrial pollution. Waste management programs are being put in place, and environmental awareness campaigns are slowly but surely changing attitudes and behaviors.

But the government cannot do it alone. Grassroots organizations and community initiatives are springing up, driven by passionate individuals fighting for a healthier future. They are raising awareness, promoting sustainable practices, and demanding stronger environmental protections.

What Can You Do?

Even if you are far away from Sindh, you can still make a difference. Support organizations working on the ground, spread awareness about the environmental challenges facing the region, and make conscious choices in your own life to reduce your environmental impact.

Sindh's struggle is a reminder that environmental pollution is not just a local issue; it's a global crisis that demands our attention and action. By working together, we can help create a healthier and more sustainable future for Sindh and the world.

Sustainable Futures: Sindh's Dance with Progress and Preservation

Imagine Sindh, the beating heart of Pakistan, as a vibrant dancer, twirling gracefully towards progress. Yet, her steps are faltering, her rhythm disrupted by the weight of environmental challenges. To find harmony, she must learn a new dance – a dance where development and nature intertwine, where economic growth and ecological balance become partners.

The Challenges: A Symphony of Strains

Sindh's dance floor is crowded. A booming population, like an ever-growing orchestra, demands more resources, more space, more energy. Cities sprawl, encroaching on fertile lands and ancient forests. The Indus River, the lifeblood of the province, weakens, its flow stifled by overuse and a changing climate. Pollution, like a discordant melody, hangs heavy in the air, water, and soil. Poverty and inequality cast long shadows, leaving many vulnerable to the harsh realities of environmental degradation.

Sustainable Development: A Choreography of Solutions

But hope is not lost. Sindh can learn a new choreography, one that embraces sustainable development. Imagine:

Solar panels gleaming like jewels on rooftops and vast deserts, harnessing the power of the sun. Windmills pirouette along the coast, generating clean energy.

Tourists marveling at the breathtaking beauty of Sindh's diverse landscapes, from the rolling sand dunes of the Thar Desert to the lush mangroves of the Indus Delta. Local communities welcome them with open arms, sharing their rich culture and traditions.

Farmers nurturing their land with organic practices, coaxing life from the soil without harming it. Water flows efficiently through fields, nourishing crops while conserving precious resources.

Cities breathing freely as green buildings rise and public transportation systems weave through the streets. Parks and gardens offer oases of calm amidst the urban bustle.

The Role of Stakeholders: A Collaborative Performance

This dance of sustainability requires many partners:

The government sets the stage, enacting strong environmental regulations, offering incentives for green initiatives, and investing in sustainable infrastructure.

Communities join the dance, sharing their wisdom, taking ownership of their resources, and leading initiatives that protect their environment.

Education becomes the conductor, raising awareness, equipping individuals with the knowledge and skills to embrace sustainability.

Practical Application: Every Step Counts

Each of us has a role to play in this grand performance:

Individuals: Reduce, reuse, recycle. Conserve water. Choose sustainable products. Support local communities. Educate yourself and others.

Businesses: Adopt eco-friendly practices. Invest in renewable energy. Support sustainable supply chains. Engage employees in sustainability initiatives.

Communities: Participate in local initiatives. Support local farmers. Promote eco-tourism. Educate future generations. Advocate for sustainable policies.

Case Studies: A Glimpse of Success

The Thar Desert Solar Park: A beacon of hope, illuminating homes with clean energy.

The Indus Delta Eco-tourism Project: Empowering communities to protect their natural heritage while sharing its beauty with the world.

The Sindh Organic Agriculture Project: Nurturing the land and the livelihoods of farmers.

Sindh's dance with progress and preservation is a complex one, but it is a dance that can lead to a brighter future. By embracing sustainable development, by working together, Sindh can find harmony, ensuring a thriving environment and a prosperous future for generations to come.

The Power of the Press: Sindhi Media and its Role in Shaping Public Discourse

A Tapestry of Voices: The Story of Sindhi Media

Imagine a vibrant tapestry woven with threads of language, culture, and history. This is the story of Sindhi media, a captivating narrative that echoes the spirit of the Sindhi people.

Early Threads: The Birth of Sindhi Journalism

In 1858, a new voice emerged in Sindh - Fawaid-ul-Akhbar, the first Sindhi newspaper. Though a government publication, it sparked a flame. Soon, newspapers like Sind Sudhar and Al-Waheed joined the chorus, championing literacy and igniting political discourse. These early publications were more than just news sources; they were platforms for a community finding its voice.

Expanding Horizons: Radio and Television

The tapestry grew richer with the advent of radio and television. In 1972, Sindh TV burst onto the scene, bringing news and entertainment in the Sindhi language. It was a watershed moment, connecting people to their culture in a new way. Radio and television became storytellers, preserving Sindhi folklore, music, and literature, and showcasing the talents of local artists.

The Digital Age: A Global Stage

The internet revolutionized the tapestry, adding intricate patterns and global connections. Websites, blogs, and social media platforms amplified Sindhi voices, creating a space for diverse perspectives and independent thought.

The world became the stage for Sindhi culture and discourse.

Challenges and Resilience

The tapestry has faced its share of storms. Censorship, political pressure, and economic constraints have threatened to fray its delicate threads. Yet, Sindhi media has persevered, demonstrating remarkable resilience.

A Future of Innovation

The future of Sindhi media is a canvas of possibilities. New technologies offer exciting avenues for growth and innovation. Imagine interactive news platforms, virtual reality experiences showcasing Sindhi heritage, and AI-powered translation tools making Sindhi content accessible to a global audience.

Preserving the Legacy: A Digital Archive

To honor this vibrant tapestry, we must preserve its history. Imagine a digital archive where historical newspapers, magazines, and audio-visual recordings are lovingly curated and made accessible to all. This would be a treasure trove for future generations, a testament to the enduring spirit of Sindhi media.

Conclusion

The story of Sindhi media is a testament to the power of language and culture to unite and inspire. It's a story of resilience, innovation, and the unwavering pursuit of truth and expression. As Sindhi media continues to evolve, it carries with it the hopes and dreams of a people, weaving a tapestry that is both timeless and ever-changing.

Subtopic 2: Representation Matters: Media's Impact on Social Perceptions

Introduction

Imagine a mirror reflecting Sindhi society. That mirror is the media – television dramas, films, newspapers, websites, and social media. But is this mirror showing a true reflection, or a distorted image? How Sindhi media portrays different groups – women, minorities, the poor – shapes how we see them and ourselves. This isn't just about entertainment; it's about power, identity, and the kind of society we want to build.

Analyzing Media Representations in Sindhi Culture

Sindhi media, like a vibrant tapestry, weaves together stories that define our culture. But who gets to be the hero, the villain, or even just a face in the crowd? Let's unravel some threads:

Women: Trapped in the Frame?

Too often, Sindhi media casts women in roles as old as the Indus River itself – the dutiful wife, the sacrificing mother, the damsel in distress. Their dreams? Their ambitions? Often relegated to the background, like whispers in the wind.

Think of those tear-jerking dramas where a woman's worth hinges on her husband's approval, her happiness sacrificed for family honor. Or those music videos where she's an object of desire, her body swaying to the rhythm, but her voice silenced. This isn't just art imitating life; it's art dictating life, reinforcing the idea that women are meant to be seen, not heard.

Minorities: Lost in the Shadows?

Sindhi society is a beautiful mosaic of different faiths, ethnicities, and languages. Yet, in our media, some pieces of this mosaic seem to be missing. Religious minorities, like Hindus and Christians, are often painted with a broad brush, their stories reduced to stereotypes. Ethnic groups like the Baloch and Pashtun are sometimes portrayed through a lens of fear and suspicion, their rich cultures overshadowed by conflict.

This invisibility and misrepresentation have real-world consequences. When we don't see ourselves reflected in the stories we consume, we feel marginalized, like we don't belong. It fuels prejudice and makes it harder to bridge divides.

Social Issues: The Unseen Scars?

Poverty, illiteracy, gender inequality – these are the open wounds of our society. Yet, Sindhi media often averts its gaze, preferring to focus on the glamorous and the powerful. This silence is deafening. It allows these problems to fester, hidden in the shadows, while those who suffer are rendered invisible.

The Ripple Effect: How Media Shapes Our Minds

The stories we consume don't just entertain; they seep into our subconscious, shaping our beliefs and attitudes. Seeing women constantly portrayed as weak and dependent can make us believe that's their rightful place. Hearing negative stereotypes about minorities can make us distrust and fear them. Ignoring social issues can make us apathetic to the suffering of others.

Turning the Tide: Media as a Force for Good

But here's the good news: media can be a powerful tool for change. Imagine Sindhi dramas where women are doctors, entrepreneurs, and leaders, breaking free from traditional roles. Imagine news reports that give a voice to the marginalized, challenging stereotypes and celebrating diversity. Imagine films that tackle social issues head-on, sparking conversations and inspiring action.

This isn't a pipe dream. It's happening, slowly but surely. Independent media outlets are pushing boundaries, telling stories that mainstream media ignores. Young filmmakers are challenging the status quo, using their art to spark dialogue. And social media is giving a platform to voices that were once silenced.

Taking Action: Building a More Inclusive Media Landscape

We all have a role to play in creating a media landscape that reflects the true face of Sindhi society. Here's how:

Become Media Literate: Learn to critically analyze what you watch and read. Question stereotypes, identify biases, and seek out diverse perspectives.

Support Responsible Media: Choose to consume content that promotes inclusion and challenges prejudice. Support independent media outlets that are telling important stories.

Amplify Marginalized Voices: Share stories that highlight the experiences of underrepresented groups. Use your own voice to challenge stereotypes and advocate for change.

Demand Better: Let media producers know that you want to see more diversity, more nuanced portrayals, and more stories that reflect the realities of Sindhi society.

Conclusion

The media isn't just a mirror; it's a window to the world we want to create. Let's use it to build a Sindhi society where everyone feels seen, heard, and valued. A society where women are empowered, minorities are celebrated, and social issues are confronted with courage and compassion. The power to shape our narrative lies within us. Let's use it wisely.

Subtopic 3: Agents of Change: Media's Role in Promoting Social Awareness and Action

The air crackles with anticipation as the familiar jingle of "Awami Awaz" fills the radio waves. From the bustling streets of Karachi to the quiet villages nestled along the Indus River, the people of Sindh tune in, eager to hear the latest news, the voices of their community, and the stories that shape their lives. In this vibrant and complex region, media isn't just a source of information, it's a catalyst for change, a mirror reflecting society's struggles and triumphs, and a powerful force pushing for a better tomorrow.

I. Raising Awareness: More Than Headlines, Human Stories

Imagine Fatima, her face etched with worry, staring at a parched field. The relentless drought has withered her crops, leaving her family with little to eat. Her story, captured by a local news crew and broadcast across Sindh, is a stark reminder of the harsh realities of climate change in the region. Sindhi media doesn't just report on statistics; it brings the human cost of these issues to life.

Poverty's Grip: We see the faces of children scavenging for scraps in overflowing garbage dumps, hear the desperate pleas of mothers unable to feed their families.

Journalists delve into the root causes of poverty, exposing systemic inequalities and demanding accountability from those in power.

A Choking Reality: The air hangs heavy with dust and fumes. Sindhi media takes us to the heart of polluted industrial zones, where residents struggle to breathe, and investigates the illegal factories operating without regard for environmental regulations.

Whispers of Injustice: In hushed tones, families share their anguish over loved ones who have vanished without a trace. Brave journalists dare to investigate these enforced disappearances, shedding light on human rights abuses and demanding justice.

Education, A Distant Dream: For many children in Sindh, especially girls, education remains a distant dream. Media outlets amplify the voices of these children, highlighting the barriers they face and advocating for equal access to quality education.

Case Study: Breaking the Silence on Forced Marriages

The wedding decorations shimmer, but behind the facade of celebration, a young girl's dreams are being crushed. Forced marriages, a deeply entrenched practice in some parts of Sindh, are brought to light through powerful documentaries like "Stolen Dreams" produced by KTN News. The film follows the harrowing journey of 16-year-old Nadia, forced to marry her cousin against her will. Her story, and the stories of others like her, sparked a public outcry and fueled a movement demanding legal reforms and support for victims.

II. Mobilizing Public Opinion: From Hashtags to Healing

A single tweet, a shared video, a powerful hashtag – in today's Sindh, social media is a potent tool for change. When a young activist's passionate speech about the lack of clean drinking water in his village goes viral, it galvanizes an entire community. Sindhi media isn't just reporting the news; it's facilitating dialogue, empowering citizens, and driving action.

Journalism with a Purpose: Investigative reports on the devastating impact of contaminated water in Tharparkar, published in the Daily Kawish, lead to public protests and force the government to take action.

Digital Uprisings: #SaveTheIndus trends on Twitter as Sindhi media uses online platforms to mobilize support for the protection of the iconic river from pollution and unsustainable development.

Citizen Voices, Citizen Power: Through online platforms like "Sindh Speaks," ordinary citizens report on issues affecting their communities, sharing stories of resilience, exposing corruption, and demanding change.

Case Study: Sindhi Media and the Fight Against Polio

The crippling fear of polio once cast a long shadow over Sindh. But through a relentless media campaign, featuring catchy Jingles, emotional appeals from mothers, and endorsements from religious leaders, the tide began to turn. Radio programs dedicated to dispelling myths about vaccination, combined with on-the-ground reporting from remote villages, helped build trust and ensure the success of the anti-polio campaign.

A Digital Battlefield: Navigating the Ethical Minefield of Sindhi Media

The digital age has transformed the media landscape into a double-edged sword. For journalists in Sindh, Pakistan, it's a battlefield where truth clashes with falsehood, and ethical journalism is under constant siege.

The Ghost in the Machine: Misinformation's Haunting Presence

Misinformation, the phantom that stalks the digital realm, has found fertile ground in Sindh. A region where a significant portion of the population relies on social media for news, it's easy for fake news to spread like wildfire, igniting social unrest and eroding trust.

Imagine a world where a simple click can turn truth into fiction. This is the reality for many Sindhis, where a rumor, amplified by the echo chamber of social media, can lead to real-world consequences. From baseless accusations to incitement of violence, the impact of misinformation can be devastating.

The Digital Gauntlet: Journalists Under Fire

Journalists, the fearless sentinels of truth, are increasingly becoming targets of online harassment and cyberbullying. The anonymity of the internet emboldens trolls to unleash a torrent of abuse, threats, and intimidation. Female journalists, in particular, find themselves at the forefront of this digital war, often facing misogynistic attacks that seek to silence their voices.

It's a chilling reality where the keyboard becomes a weapon, and every keystroke is a potential bullet aimed at a journalist's reputation and mental well-being. The fear of online harassment can stifle critical reporting, leading to a chilling effect on freedom of expression.

A Fractured Mirror: The Lack of Diversity and Representation

Sindhi media, like a fractured mirror, often fails to reflect the diverse tapestry of the region. Marginalized communities and perspectives are frequently overlooked, perpetuating social inequalities. The digital divide further exacerbates this issue, as many in rural areas lack access to technology and the digital literacy skills needed to navigate the online world.

It's a stark reality where the voices of the marginalized are silenced, and the dominant narrative shapes public opinion. A more diverse and inclusive media landscape is essential to ensure that all voices are heard and that a more accurate representation of society is portrayed.

The Siren Song of Sensationalism: The Temptation of Clickbait

In the relentless pursuit of clicks and ad revenue, media outlets often succumb to the siren song of sensationalism. Clickbait headlines, exaggerated claims, and distorted truths can erode public trust and undermine the credibility of journalism.

It's a constant struggle between ethics and economics, where the temptation to prioritize profit over principle can be overwhelming. However, a responsible media must resist the allure of sensationalism and prioritize accuracy, fairness, and objectivity.

The Digital Divide: A Barrier to Information and Empowerment

The digital divide, a chasm that separates the connected from the disconnected, poses a significant challenge to media ethics in Sindh. Limited access to technology and digital literacy skills can leave many vulnerable to misinformation and disinformation.

It's a stark reminder that the digital age is not a level playing field. Bridging the digital divide is essential to ensure that everyone has equal access to information and the tools to critically evaluate it.

A Call to Action: Reclaiming the Digital Frontier

To navigate the ethical minefield of the digital age, media organizations and journalists must unite to reclaim the digital frontier. By embracing fact-checking, promoting media literacy, protecting journalists, and fostering diversity and inclusion, we can create a more ethical and responsible media landscape.

It's a collective responsibility to ensure that the digital age is not just a technological revolution, but a moral one as well. By upholding the highest ethical standards, we can safeguard the integrity of journalism and empower citizens to make informed decisions.

The future of media ethics in Sindh is in our hands. Let's choose the path of truth, justice, and responsible journalism.

.

Entrepreneurial Spirit: Sindhi Business Communities and Economic Development

Subtopic 1: A Legacy of Trade: Historical Overview of Sindhi Business Communities

Introduction

Imagine a people whose history is interwoven with the very fabric of trade, their entrepreneurial spirit as ancient as the Indus River that cradles their homeland. The Sindhi business community, a vibrant tapestry of resilience and innovation, has for millennia played a pivotal role in the economic development of Sindh and beyond. Their story is one of adaptation, community, and a relentless pursuit of prosperity.

Historical Roots: Whispers of the Indus

The roots of Sindhi commerce delve deep into the mists of time, echoing back to the bustling marketplaces of the Indus Valley Civilization. These ancient Sindhis, skilled artisans and shrewd traders, established intricate trade routes that snaked through the region, connecting them with distant civilizations. Their legacy of commercial prowess endured through the ages, as Sindh evolved into a vital crossroads in the heart of a dynamic trade network spanning India, Central Asia, and the Middle East.

Navigating the Colonial Tide

During the era of British colonialism, Sindhi businessmen emerged as key architects of the region's economic landscape. With remarkable adaptability, they navigated the complexities of the colonial system, establishing thriving enterprises in diverse sectors such as textiles, banking, and shipping. The Sindhi diaspora, driven by an insatiable entrepreneurial spirit, extended its reach across the globe, planting the seeds of prosperity in new lands.

Shaping Economies: A Sindhi Touch

The contributions of Sindhi business communities to economic development resonate far and wide. Their ventures have spanned a vast spectrum of industries, from the clattering looms of textile mills to the bustling aisles of retail stores, from the towering cranes of shipping yards to the humming machinery of manufacturing plants.

The establishment of the Bombay Stock Exchange in 1875 stands as a testament to their enduring impact. This iconic institution, now a global financial powerhouse, bears the indelible mark of Sindhi entrepreneurship. Similarly, the National Bank of Pakistan, founded in 1949, has played a pivotal role in shaping Pakistan's economy, a testament to the Sindhi community's commitment to nation-building.

The Sindhi Entrepreneur: A Portrait of Success

What is the secret behind the enduring success of Sindhi entrepreneurs? Their story is one of resilience, adaptability, and an unwavering commitment to community.

   Adaptability: Like seasoned sailors navigating treacherous waters, Sindhi entrepreneurs have weathered the storms of changing economic climates, adjusting their sails to harness new opportunities.
   Community Bonds: The Sindhi community is a tightly woven tapestry of support, where family and friends serve as anchors, offering guidance and encouragement in the face of challenges.

Unwavering Determination: Sindhi entrepreneurs are renowned for their work ethic, their willingness to burn the midnight oil and make sacrifices in pursuit of their dreams.

Preserving the Legacy: A Tapestry of Stories

Imagine a historical exhibition that breathes life into the rich tapestry of Sindhi business history. Visitors wander through interactive displays, tracing the footsteps of these remarkable entrepreneurs from the ancient markets of the Indus Valley to the bustling trading floors of modern stock exchanges.

Or perhaps a documentary film, capturing the essence of the Sindhi entrepreneurial spirit through intimate interviews with business leaders, historians, and community members. These stories, interwoven with archival footage and vibrant visuals, paint a compelling portrait of a community that has left an indelible mark on the world.

Conclusion

The Sindhi business community's journey Is an epic tale of resilience, adaptability, and unwavering community support. Their entrepreneurial spirit, passed down through generations, continues to shape economies and inspire aspiring business leaders. By celebrating their rich history and invaluable contributions, we ensure that their legacy continues to illuminate the path towards a more prosperous future.

Additional Resources

To further explore the fascinating world of Sindhi business communities, consider these resources:

Books: Search for titles like "The Sindhi Merchants: A History of Entrepreneurship" or "Sindh: Land of Opportunity" in libraries or online bookstores.

Academic Journals: Explore journals specializing in South Asian history, economics, or business studies for in-depth research articles on Sindhi business communities.

Community Organizations: Connect with Sindhi cultural centers or business associations for firsthand accounts and insights into their rich heritage.

2. The Sindhi Spirit: From Indus Valley to Global Boardrooms

The Indus Valley civilization, one of the world's oldest, laid the foundation for a culture that would later give rise to a remarkable entrepreneurial spirit. Sindhis, descendants of this ancient civilization, have carried this entrepreneurial torch through centuries, illuminating industries and economies worldwide.

2.1 Icons of Industry: The Sindhi Mavericks

The Hinduja Brothers: A Tapestry Woven in Gold: More than just billionaires, the Hinduja brothers are architects of a global conglomerate. Their journey, from humble beginnings in Sindh to dominating industries like banking, oil, and media, is a testament to their unwavering vision and strategic acumen.

Anil Ambani: The Maverick Who Redefined Connectivity: This bold entrepreneur revolutionized India's telecommunications landscape. His audacious ventures and relentless pursuit of innovation have cemented his legacy as a visionary.

Nirmala Sitharaman: A Woman of Substance: Breaking glass ceilings, Sitharaman's ascent to the pinnacle of Indian finance is an inspiration. Her sharp intellect, unwavering determination, and astute economic policies have made her a force to be reckoned with.

Azim Premji: The Tech Titan with a Heart of Gold: Beyond his role as a tech mogul, Premji is a philanthropist extraordinaire. His commitment to education and social causes has left an indelible mark on Indian society.

Ritesh Agarwal: The Young Disruptor: A millennial marvel, Agarwal's OYO Rooms disrupted the hospitality industry. His innovative approach and relentless drive have made him a symbol of youthful entrepreneurial energy.

2.2 The Secret Sauce: Unraveling the Sindhi Entrepreneurial DNA

What sets Sindhi entrepreneurs apart? It's a unique blend of traits:

Risk-takers by Nature: With a fearless spirit, Sindhis embrace uncertainty, daring to venture into uncharted territories.

Born Entrepreneurs: The entrepreneurial bug runs deep in their veins, an innate ability to spot opportunities and turn them into thriving ventures.

Community-Centric: Sindhis understand the power of collective strength. Their businesses often serve as catalysts for social and economic development.

Family First: Strong family ties provide the bedrock of support, fostering a sense of belonging and shared purpose.

Adaptability: Like the Indus River, Sindhis are adaptable, navigating the ever-changing tides of business with grace and resilience.

2.3 A Diverse Tapestry: Sindhi Ventures Across Industries

Sindhi entrepreneurs have made significant contributions to a wide range of sectors:

Textiles: Weaving Dreams into Reality: From traditional handlooms to cutting-edge textile technologies, Sindhis have shaped the global fashion industry.

Jewelry: Crafting Timeless Beauty: Renowned for their exquisite craftsmanship, Sindhi jewelers have adorned royalty and celebrities alike.

Software and Technology: Pioneering the Digital Age: From Silicon Valley to India's tech hubs, Sindhi entrepreneurs have driven innovation and digital transformation.

Finance and Banking: Masters of finance, Sindhis have built financial empires that span continents.

Real Estate: Shaping Urban Landscapes: With a keen eye for real estate, Sindhis have developed iconic properties and transformed city skylines.

Healthcare: Healing the World: Driven by a passion for healthcare, Sindhis have established world-class hospitals and medical institutions.

Education: Nurturing Future Leaders: Investing in education, Sindhis have founded prestigious schools and universities.

2.4 Fostering the Next Generation: Mentorship and Networking

To empower the next generation of Sindhi entrepreneurs, mentorship and networking play a crucial role. Organizations like the Sindhi Chamber of Commerce and Industry, the Sindhi Foundation, and various community groups provide invaluable support and resources. By fostering a vibrant entrepreneurial ecosystem, we can ensure that the Sindhi spirit continues to thrive and shape the future.

The legacy of Sindhi entrepreneurship is a testament to the power of human ingenuity, resilience, and the pursuit of excellence. As we celebrate their achievements, let us also inspire the next generation of dreamers and doers to carry forward this rich heritage.

Fostering Innovation: Igniting the Entrepreneurial Spirit in Sindh

Imagine a Sindh where vibrant new businesses sprout up like desert flowers after a rain, where young minds brimming with ideas find fertile ground to cultivate their dreams. This is the vision of a Sindh empowered by entrepreneurship, a driving force for economic growth and development.

While Sindh's entrepreneurial landscape shows glimmers of promise with initiatives like the Sindh Enterprise Development Fund (SEDF) and the Sindh Business Development Centre (SBDC), it's like a garden yearning for more sunlight and nourishment. Aspiring entrepreneurs face challenges akin to navigating a thorny path: limited access to finance, a lack of essential business skills, and the struggle to reach eager markets.

Breaking Barriers, Building Bridges

To truly unleash Sindh's entrepreneurial potential, we need to break down these barriers and build bridges to opportunity. Imagine:

A Financial Oasis: Microloans and grants become readily available, like refreshing springs in the desert, quenching the thirst of startups for capital.
Skill-Building Caravans: Traveling workshops and mentorship programs traverse the province, imparting invaluable business knowledge and empowering entrepreneurs with the tools for success.

Market Bazaars: Vibrant online platforms and bustling trade fairs connect Sindh's entrepreneurs with a global audience, showcasing their unique products and services.

Cultivating a Culture of Innovation

But it's not just about resources; it's about fostering a mindset, a culture that celebrates risk-taking and creative thinking. Imagine:

Innovation Hubs: Co-working spaces and incubators buzz with energy, where entrepreneurs collaborate, share ideas, and learn from each other's journeys.

University Seedbeds: Entrepreneurship courses become embedded in university curricula, nurturing the next generation of innovators and changemakers.

Government as a Gardener: Policies bloom that incentivize innovation, providing tax breaks and grants for research and development, like fertile soil for groundbreaking ideas.

Harnessing the Power of Technology

In this digital age, technology can be a powerful ally for Sindh's entrepreneurs. Imagine:

E-commerce Camels: Online platforms become the trusty steeds of Sindh's entrepreneurs, carrying their wares to far-off markets with ease.

Social Media Oases: Entrepreneurs leverage the power of social media to connect with customers, build communities, and tell their stories to the world.

Mobile Money Caravans: Digital payment solutions empower entrepreneurs, especially women, in remote areas, enabling them to participate fully in the economy.

A Collective Effort

Fostering entrepreneurship in Sindh is not a solo endeavor; it requires a collective effort, a symphony of government support, educational institutions, and private sector initiatives. Together, they can create an ecosystem where entrepreneurial dreams take flight and soar.

By investing in Sindh's entrepreneurs, we invest in the future of the province, creating jobs, boosting the economy, and empowering individuals to build a better life for themselves and their communities. Let's ignite the entrepreneurial spirit in Sindh and watch it illuminate the path to a brighter tomorrow.

Beyond Profit: Where the Heart of Business Beats

Forget dry statistics and corporate jargon. We're diving into the heart of what truly matters: how Sindhi businesses are weaving compassion and social responsibility into the very fabric of their work. This isn't just about ticking boxes; it's about a deep-rooted belief in giving back, a legacy passed down through generations.

A Legacy of Generosity

Imagine bustling bazaars in the Sindh region, centuries ago. Merchants, with their keen sense of trade, also understood the importance of community. This wasn't just about profit; it was about ensuring everyone had a chance to thrive. This spirit lives on in modern Sindhi businesses, where social responsibility isn't an afterthought, it's in their DNA.

Planting Seeds of Change: Education

Think of a young girl in a rural village, her eyes bright with dreams. But poverty casts a long shadow, threatening to extinguish her hopes for education. Enter a Sindhi business, not with a handout, but with a hand up. They build a school, a beacon of knowledge, where she and countless others can learn and grow. This isn't charity; it's an investment in the future, a belief that education can break the cycle of poverty and empower generations to come.

Healing Hands: Healthcare

Picture a remote community, where healthcare is a luxury, not a right. Illness casts a pall of fear, and treatable diseases become life-threatening. But then, a lifeline arrives. A Sindhi business steps in, funding a new clinic, bringing doctors and medicine to those who need it most. This isn't just about treating illnesses; it's about restoring hope and giving people a chance at a healthy life.

When Disaster Strikes: A Beacon of Hope

Imagine a town ravaged by floods, homes destroyed, lives shattered. Amidst the chaos, a familiar sight emerges: trucks bearing the logo of a Sindhi company, laden with supplies, food, and medicine. This isn't just about corporate responsibility; it's about human compassion, about standing with those in need when they need it most.

Beyond Charity: Building Thriving Communities

This isn't just about writing checks; it's about rolling up sleeves and getting involved. Sindhi businesses are revitalizing communities, building roads, supporting local artisans, and creating a ripple effect of positive change. They understand that a thriving community benefits everyone, creating a virtuous cycle of prosperity and well-being.

The Khimji Ramdas Group: A Legacy in Oman

In the heart of Oman, the Khimji Ramdas Group isn't just building businesses; they're building a legacy. From supporting schools that nurture young minds to funding hospitals that provide life-saving care, they're deeply woven into the fabric of Omani society. Their commitment to environmental sustainability, like their initiative to plant thousands of trees, shows a vision that extends beyond profit, towards a greener, healthier future for all.

Challenges and the Road Ahead

The journey isn't without its challenges. How do we measure the true impact of these efforts? How do we ensure these values are embraced by the next generation of leaders? These are questions that Sindhi businesses are grappling with, seeking innovative ways to scale their impact and create a lasting legacy of positive change.

Social Entrepreneurship: Where Passion Meets Purpose

Imagine a world where business isn't just about the bottom line, but about solving the world's most pressing problems. This is the world of social entrepreneurship, where passion and purpose collide. These aren't just businesses; they're engines of social change, tackling poverty, inequality, and environmental degradation head-on.

SELCO India: Lighting Up Lives

In rural India, where darkness often means a standstill, SELCO India is bringing light and opportunity. They're not just selling solar panels; they're empowering communities. Imagine a small village, once shrouded in darkness, now illuminated by clean energy, where children can study at night, and businesses can thrive. This is the transformative power of social entrepreneurship, where profit fuels purpose.

A Call to Action: Join the Movement

This isn't just a story about Sindhi businesses; it's a call to action for all of us. How can we support businesses that prioritize people and planet? How can we nurture the next generation of social entrepreneurs? The answers lie in our choices, our investments, and our commitment to a world where business is a force for good.

About Sindhi Author

Early Life and Education

Azhar ul Haque Sario's story isn't just about degrees and achievements—it's about a boy from Karachi who found magic in the pages of books. Imagine young Azhar, lost in worlds both real and fantastical, his imagination fueled by stories that whispered of faraway lands and incredible possibilities. This early love for literature, nurtured by his educator parents, blossomed into a lifelong passion for writing.

His journey to Cambridge was like stepping into a whole new universe. Picture him navigating the hallowed halls of this prestigious university, exchanging ideas with brilliant minds from all corners of the globe. This experience wasn't just about academics; it was about expanding his worldview, challenging his perspectives, and forging connections that would last a lifetime.

But Azhar's story takes an unexpected turn. He returns to Pakistan, not to pursue a literary career, but to delve into the corporate world. Yet, his thirst for knowledge remains unquenched. He conquers MBAs, ACCA qualifications, and BBA degrees, showcasing his relentless drive and intellectual curiosity.

And then, something remarkable happens. Azhar discovers the captivating world of data science. Imagine him, amidst spreadsheets and algorithms, uncovering hidden patterns and unlocking the secrets held within complex datasets. This fascination stems from a research project during his MBA, where he witnessed firsthand the power of data to shape strategies and drive informed decisions.

Azhar's journey is a testament to the multifaceted nature of human potential. He's a testament to the idea that we can be both poets and analysts, storytellers and data scientists. His story is an inspiration, a reminder that our paths may twist and turn, but our passions, once ignited, can lead us to extraordinary destinations.

A Prolific Writing Career

Azhar ul Haque Sario isn't just a writer; he's a writing machine! This man has penned over 2810 books – yes, you read that right – on topics ranging from the history of Pakistan to the mysteries of the cosmos. Imagine him hunched over his keyboard, fueled by endless cups of chai, churning out page after page with the relentless energy of a runaway train.

Sario's journey is like a literary odyssey. He started with textbooks, explaining the intricacies of biology and the secrets of successful sales forecasting. But then, like a caterpillar transforming into a butterfly, he spread his wings and took flight into the world of fiction. He whisked readers away on thrilling adventures in "The London Chronicles," explored the complexities of love and loss in his (still secret!) romance novels, and even delved into the minds of young adults in his yet-to-be-revealed YA series.

This guy is a genre chameleon! One day he's dissecting the "Anatomy of Economic Inequality," the next he's waxing poetic in "Resonance of Existence." He even offers spiritual guidance in his book on the Prophet Muhammad (PBUH). It's like he has a different hat for every genre, and he wears them all with remarkable flair.

But what makes Sario's writing tick? It's his ability to connect. He writes with clarity and conciseness, like a master craftsman chiseling away at a block of marble to reveal the beauty within. He sprinkles his work with stories and anecdotes, making even the most complex topics come alive. He's like that teacher who could make even the most boring subject fascinating, drawing you in with their passion and enthusiasm.

Sario's books are like a mirror reflecting the human experience. He explores themes of personal growth, the thirst for knowledge, the clash and harmony of cultures, and the fight for a better world. He wants you to learn, to grow, to question, and to dream.

And the world has taken notice! In 2024, Sario was honored by the Asia Books of Records for his mind-boggling literary output. It's like winning an Olympic gold medal for writing! This recognition not only celebrates Sario's individual achievement but also shines a spotlight on Pakistan's vibrant literary scene.

Azhar ul Haque Sario is more than just a writer; he's a phenomenon. He's a testament to the power of dedication, versatility, and a boundless imagination. He shows us that with passion and perseverance, we can achieve extraordinary things. So next time you're looking for a good read, dive into the world of Sario. You might just find yourself getting lost in the sheer volume and variety of his work, marveling at the boundless energy of this literary dynamo.

Bridging Data Science and Storytelling

Imagine a writer who can make numbers sing and algorithms dance. That's Azhar ul Haque Sario. He's not your typical data scientist, hunched over spreadsheets in a dimly lit room. No, Sario wields data like a poet wields words, crafting narratives that both illuminate and entertain.

Think of him as a Sherlock Holmes of the digital age, sifting through the clues hidden within datasets, but instead of solving crimes, he's unlocking the secrets of the universe. He can take the cold, hard facts of sales forecasting and turn them into a thrilling tale of market trends and consumer behavior. Or he can delve into the ethereal realm of quantum computing, making the complex dance of qubits understandable and even captivating.

Sario's writing is like a magic trick. He takes something that seems dry and inaccessible – data – and transforms it into something vibrant and engaging. He's a master of weaving information and storytelling, creating a tapestry where numbers and narratives intertwine.

His books aren't just textbooks or reports; they're journeys of discovery. In "Growing Sindh Wealth," he doesn't just present statistics; he paints a picture of a region on the rise, its people striving for a better future. In "Health Tech Revolution," he takes us to the cutting edge of medicine, where technology and biology merge to combat disease and enhance human life.

Sario's unique gift is his ability to bridge the gap between the analytical and the creative. He's a translator of sorts, converting the language of data into the language of human experience. He doesn't just inform; he inspires. He doesn't just educate; he enlightens.

So, the next time you encounter a complex dataset, don't just see a jumble of numbers. Think of Azhar ul Haque Sario, and imagine the story hidden within, waiting to be revealed.

A Sindhi Voice on the Global Stage

The aroma of freshly brewed chai hung heavy in the air, mingling with the scent of old books and whispered prayers. A young Azhar, curled up in a corner of his grandfather's library, devoured tales of ancient Sindhi heroes and Sufi mystics. This thirst for knowledge, nurtured in the heart of Sindh, would later propel him on an extraordinary journey, a global odyssey fueled by the spirit of his homeland.

Azhar ul Haque Sario, a name now synonymous with intellectual curiosity and prolific writing, carries the soul of Sindh within him. His journey, spanning over 190 books and countless articles, is a testament to the power of cultural identity to transcend borders and inspire minds across the globe.

"My roots are deeply embedded in the soil of Sindh," Sario once confessed in a rare interview, "but my branches reach out to embrace the world." And embrace it he does. His works, a vibrant tapestry of diverse subjects, reflect this global outlook.

Imagine a student in Karachi, poring over Sario's "Cambridge O Level Biology 5090," her dreams of becoming a doctor taking flight with every page. Picture a young entrepreneur in London, finding solace and inspiration in "The Art of Falling Upward," its message of resilience echoing in his heart as he navigates the challenges of a startup. Visualize a scholar in New York, engrossed in "Diplomacy over War: Islamic Perspective," Sario's words offering a fresh perspective on conflict resolution in a turbulent world.

Sario's writings are not mere collections of words; they are bridges connecting cultures, sparking dialogue, and empowering individuals. He doesn't shy away from tackling complex issues, from the intricacies of quantum computing in "Quantum Horizons Unleashed" to the ethical dilemmas of merging biology and technology in "Health Tech Revolution." He delves into the depths of human existence in "Resonance of Existence," inviting readers on a journey of introspection and self-discovery.

But perhaps his most profound contribution lies in his ability to weave the threads of his Sindhi heritage into his diverse body of work. His "Pakistan History" is not just a chronological account of events; it's a nuanced exploration of the nation's past, seen through the eyes of a Sindhi son. His biography of "Muhammad Ali Jinnah" offers a fresh perspective on the founder of Pakistan, highlighting the complexities of his leadership and the challenges of nation-building.

Azhar ul Haque Sario may not be a writer of Sindhi folklore or poetry, but he is undoubtedly a Sindhi voice on the global stage. His journey, a testament to the power of education, the resilience of the human spirit, and the enduring strength of cultural identity, serves as an inspiration to aspiring writers and thinkers around the world. He reminds us that our roots, no matter how deep or far-reaching, can nourish our dreams and shape our destinies.

So, let us celebrate this remarkable author, this global citizen with a Sindhi soul, and delve into the rich tapestry of his work. For in his writings, we discover not only the brilliance of a single mind, but also the echoes of a vibrant culture and the aspirations of a people.

www.ingramcontent.com/pod-product-compliance
Ingram Content Group UK Ltd.
Pitfield, Milton Keynes, MK11 3LW, UK
UKHW021059260125
454178UK00004B/310